The Human Conspiracy

Nigel Calder

The Human Conspiracy

British Broadcasting Corporation

Published by the
British Broadcasting Corporation
35 Marylebone High Street
London W1M 4AA

ISBN 0 563 12888 7

First published 1976

Printed in England by
Lowe and Brydone (Printers) Ltd
Thetford, Norfolk

Author's note
This book is a product of world-wide interactions with men and women working at frontiers of research into human social behaviour. It accompanies a television programme written for the BBC and its overseas co-producers and I am grateful for the travelling opportunities provided in that connection. The book draws and enlarges upon information gathered for the programme but is separately conceived and written. I am sorry that I cannot acknowledge, properly and individually, all of the 150 experts who gave unstinted help and advice; although the work of only a minority of them is described in the pages that follow, everyone contributed to the general perspective.

(Overleaf) 'The Fight between Carnival and Lent', by Pieter Brueghel.

Contents

The 120-minute television programme *The Human Conspiracy* was first transmitted on BBC2 on 6 December 1975. It was made by the BBC as a coproduction with WNET (New York), SR1 (Stockholm), KRO (Hilversum) and BRT (Brussels). The executive producer was Alec Nisbett, assisted by Martin Freeth. John Hooper was the principal film cameraman and the film editor was Christopher Woolley. Graphics were by Alan Jeapes and visual effects by Tony Oxley. Stewart Marshall was the studio designer and studio direction was by Brian Johnson. The programme was presented by Caroline Medawar, narrated by Eric Porter and written by Nigel Calder.

Introduction

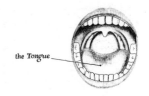

the Tongue

Put out your tongue at a baby. Provided he is not fretful, fearful or in any of the other distracted states in which human beings spend much of their early life, the chances are good that he will put out his tongue right back at you. Babies less than a week old are capable of this reaction. Few of the men of learning who have written about human nature over the past few thousand years, right down to the 1970s, can have performed this simple experiment. They cannot even have looked closely at babies at all; had they done so, we might have been spared a good deal of nonsense.

The experiment with tongues is a simple observation with dramatic implications. It ranks with watching a ship disappearing below the horizon and deducing that the world is round; or suspecting from the snug fit of the coastlines of Africa and South America that those continents have drifted apart; or reasoning from the darkness of the night sky that our universe is probably finite in extent. The baby who retaliates with his tongue is making several cardinal statements:

He recognises another human being when he sees one and he is willing spontaneously to attend to what the other is doing. When you extend your tongue the baby in some sense knows to what part of his own body that fleshy organ corresponds. He also shows that he can work the muscles in order to imitate the action. But the baby is innocent of any instruction in tonguework and of any practice in front of a mirror. Least of all does he need any schedule of rewards or punishments, either to shape his competence in this exchange of tongue signals or to motivate him for the effort it involves.

Out of the mouth of the babe comes a gesture that older people interpret as being rude. It is well directed at those sages who declare that a newborn baby is empty-headed – a clean slate on which society must write everything, or a puppet to be manipulated by behavioural engineers. The protruding tongue would be an appropriate comment on behaviourism, the school of psychology that knew of nothing except learning and which hobbled the human sciences for half a century. But the baby has no evident intention of being rude. The genes of human heredity that have wired his brain with a prior knowledge of faces and tongues leave him uninstructed in the social meaning of tongue-poking.

There, the child does have a great deal to learn. For instance he must find out that the same tongue safely used among children as a signal of transient insolence may provoke wrath if extended towards any adult other than a physician. If he happens to have been born in India, where holy men slit their tongues and then display the unpleasant pink duality as proof of fortitude, the child will in due course learn this further codicil of social meanings. He will be an apt pupil, because the organisation of his brain makes it easy for him to attend to and master the nuances of human behaviour, never mind what kind of dunce he may turn out to be when it comes to algebra or Latin declensions. Opinions at the other extreme from behaviourism will not do, either. Human babies are not reluctant learners whose brutish instincts must be curbed before they are fit to be allowed out in public.

People are predisposed to learn to be civilised. Why and how that happens, and why in spite of it our human world is noted for its adult sins and follies – these are the primary questions that this book addresses. They are ancient issues, of course, but today people tremble with better reason than ever for the future of our world. The science that erodes old faiths and reluctantly puts fearsome weapons in the hands of fallible old men must now attend properly to human nature. The issues have often been approached in a moralising or cynical mood, perhaps with the aim of proving some ideological point. For science the proper mood is wonder.

Isaac Newton was by all accounts an irritable fellow but if he had watched the ever-changing moon as peevishly as the observers of the social scene regard their fellow humans he would have offered a treatise on the unreliability of the lighting at night, rather than a law of gravity. Charles Darwin was a hypochondriac gentleman, fearful of the outcry that would greet his findings, and he did not arrive at the principle of evolution by natural selection in any spirit of reformist zeal. He was first and foremost a man enchanted by living things, who would climb mountains to marvel at the pretty beasts and fossils they concealed. Even in an age of H-bombs and neglected famines, it is not escapist to declare that we should begin an inquiry into human nature with a gasp of wonder at the baby who stuck out his tongue. If that is not impressive, everything else that babies actually do may remain unregarded. Then there may be no check on the different kinds of fallacies about what babies and other humans are like, that are cherished by the warring ideologies.

Without an adequate sense of wonder that humans exist at all, as products of nature able to reflect upon and research into their own existence, we take salient and vulnerable features of our humanity too much for granted. In a crowded country, human heads seem two a penny. Yet the human brain is the most remarkable object within our ken, and that ken now reaches across billions of light-years to the very boundary of the universe and through aeons that extend back till long before the Sun and its family of planets were formed. On such a time scale humans made their appearance only in the last few moments, as animals distinguished by clever brains, clever hands and unusual sociability.

In earlier books I have dealt with current research on the physical and biological backgrounds of our existence, and with what is known so far about the living machinery of the brain. If the time seems ripe to report on the science of human social behaviour it is not because there is a complete and definitive body of knowledge waiting to be retailed. It is rather that, after a succession of false starts, such a science at last seems to be functioning. In contrast with simple-minded theories of the recent past, it allows that any human being is a magnificently complex product of millions of years of biology and a lifetime's social experience. Given the proper sense of wonder, discoveries are beginning to flow.

I have had a special opportunity to meet many of the leading investigators and to hear from them at first hand about the new directions in research. Like various of its predecessors, this book is one product of a joint enterprise involving the British Broadcasting Corporation and television organisations in several other countries. Because we were making a television co-production Alec Nisbett of the BBC and I were able to visit biologists, psychologists and social scientists in a dozen countries around the world, and also to spend a little time in 'stone-age' villages of Papua New Guinea. Not all of the experts whom we consulted were sympathetic to the notion of a new science emerging; for some the old approaches were good enough and this book may well be execrable for them. But plenty of others were willing to affirm a sense of progress towards a less blinkered view of humankind.

The searchers

After wonder, richness. The fossil-hunter who sieves the sediments of Africa for traces of our early human ancestors wants to know what kind of people they were, the better to understand what we ourselves are really like. The animal behaviourist who stalks a family of monkeys through the rain forest is seeking principles of social relationships that may somehow apply to our-

selves. Holding another mirror to man, the anthropologist confers with an exotic tribe, trying to make sense of its bizarre and bewildering customs. In maternity hospitals and nurseries, psychologists and linguists explore the mind of the growing child, as he gradually matures into a sociable human being. Some researchers into adult behaviour detachedly observe the characteristic gestures and ploys of human individuals interacting face-to-face. Others put students through a deceptive test, to see how their group loyalties affect their judgements. What rich material here, for picturing ourselves!

Along with biologists, physicians, psychologists and social scientists of other kinds, all these people have a common and noble end in view. They are all searching for the roots of our behaviour, for a better grasp of human nature. Almost all of them believe that such knowledge will be worth having, because it will eventually help our species to live more wisely and perhaps even silence the guns. Yet each brings to his work a specialist bent, which reflects his own skills, interests and prejudices. And he is all too easily entranced by what his own methods disclose. The brain researcher, dextrous with the knife, the microelectrode or the micropipette, is tempted to see the wiring of the brain as the key to everything. The anthropologist, on the other hand, may read over his notes by a hurricane lamp and postulate that the formulas of marriage must illuminate all our lives. But the view of mankind that these or any other single-minded approaches can offer is by definition limited, a caricature from which most of the interesting features are missing.

Until recently a galleryful of caricatures, no two of them alike and none of them recognisably human, was all that science had to show for many decades of devoted research. Despite the glaring discrepancies, each cartoonist stood proudly in front of his offering and scorned the work of others. So the sex-maniac hung there, obsessed with his orifices and lusting for his mother with death in his heart. Nearby was the naked ape with the killer instinct, hating his own kind as no animal had done before. At the far end of the gallery were various empty-headed people, waiting listlessly to be set in motion by conditioned reflexes or economic forces. Along the walls were many others: for instance, a recent survey described twenty serious and competing theories of personality, including the theory that personality does not exist. An outsider, the ordinary human being visiting this gallery to see himself portrayed, would be entitled to remark that none of the caricatures looked capable of building memorable civilisations. He might well wonder when all the artists would start comparing notes.

Simple prejudice, political as well as professional, was the great barrier to mutual understanding. All research on human behaviour raises political issues, ranging from questions of what studies are ethical to the ideological implications of the findings. Many biology experts wanted to prove that our behaviour is programmed by our genes. To others that smelt of Social Darwinism, which had nothing to do with Darwin but a lot to do with the notions that the poor are born to be poor and that some races are better than others. By reaction, these other experts denied to biology any important part in our behaviour and set up the model of empty-headed babies moulded by experience. Reconciliation was the last thing that the warring academics had in mind, as they went on rehearsing their predelictions in the name of science. And yet if only there could be a little cooling of attitudes, a certain readiness to admit that biology and culture both play important and inseparable parts in influencing our conduct, revelations might come.

If science would speak to science, if all those bright people looking into all those fascinating aspects of behaviour would get together, could they not put together a lifelike portrait of a human being, full of richness and subtlety? Happily, such a reunion is in progress in our time. Observers of the human social scene draw inspiration from the methods of the ethologists, the students of animal behaviour. Sophisticated biologists, in their turn, focus on the extraordinary *differences* in social behaviour between humans and other animals, and on the rise of culture. Instead of looking for superficial similarities between man and beast they are beginning to quote the sociologists and social anthropologists. The old issue of nature and nurture, of whether genes or circumstances shape the performance of individuals and populations, is resolving itself, not in an unhelpful generalisation about 'a little of each' but in precise studies of their interplay in particular aspects of behaviour. Specialists concerned with genes, bodies, brains or societies are coming out of their corners, opening their minds and uncovering new information about why people think and behave as they do.

The genius of infants must take a lot of the credit for breaking down the old enmities between the scientists. The small humans kept doing things they were not supposed to be able to do, according to this or that theory. It is in the nursery that the new unified science of human behaviour seems most real and effective, and most quickly rid of old and sterile conflicts. For investigators into infancy, the key word nowadays is 'interaction'. It is aptly ambiguous because it can refer either to the interaction of the child's biological endowment and the circumstances of his life, or to the child interacting with other humans, notably his mother.

At last, networks of ideas connect diverse researches that span human affairs through all ages of life. This book does not purport to sum up the human science of our time (who could do that?) or to deal exhaustively with any single topic. Instead the aim is to follow a path through the network which brings us upon a sufficiency of unexpected and important findings and ideas. It will cover enough ground to give some impression of where current research is leading us, as it explores social behaviour in our ancestors, our children and ourselves. In the process, science's portrait of the human being will become more recognisable.

A price has to be paid, though, in a loss of confidence in overarching theories. For instance Karl Marx, Sigmund Freud, Claude Lévi-Strauss, B. F. Skinner and Konrad Lorenz have all offered broad accounts of human nature or human society, which are now found wanting in central respects. Even the work of Jean Piaget, which covers many aspects of mental and social life in a coherent account of the development of children, does not find universal acceptance as a basis for the current science. Apart from the Darwinian view, which may be altogether too accommodating, there is nothing in sight to replace these earlier theories; certainly nothing that spans the biological, developmental and sociological views of man. Serge Moscovici in Paris has even pleaded for a 'phlogiston' theory of social psychology, by analogy with the false explanation of combustion that chemists at one time found useful. He would sooner have that than no theory at all.

Fragments of new theory crop up in this book, but on the whole the subject is back, perhaps where it belongs, in a 'natural history' phase. Theory waits on facts and scientists strive to observe with new precision the complexities of human behaviour. Much of what they are finding can be summed up in the metaphor of the human conspiracy.

The conspirators

People make people, not just by breeding them but **by** shaping one another's behaviour. They conspire to en-

Careful scrutiny of what people actually do in public helps to make the scientific portrait of the human being more recognisable.

The readiness with which human beings conspire together in groups, large or small, is the source of the greatest achievem
and the greatest follies.

courage proper behaviour and to check what is improper. Customs differ but the need for customs is universal. This arose, as Chapter 1 will discuss, in the course of our common evolution from our apelike ancestors. First evolution permitted our forebears to become extraordinarily sociable animals. Sociability became compulsory as human beings shed the refined but inflexible animal competences we call instinct and were obliged to learn from one another how to behave.

We conspire or perish. Chapter 2 describes how a baby arrives in the world as a ready conspirator, primed to be friendly, and predisposed to acquire the ways of his culture. From the earliest weeks the baby is actively responding to the sounds and cadences of human speech, and engaging in quasi-conversational exercises with his mother. Play becomes an important aid to mastering the rules of life and language. There are individual differences affecting these human interactions, including variations in the temperament of babies, which are determined, in part, by heredity. Yet, as considered in Chapter 3, cultural factors can influence the way people think, and even affect their perception of the world.

As a child grows bigger, he is drawn into a broader conspiracy. Chapter 4 opens with the children who between six and puberty spontaneously form an autonomous society of their own; it is replete with rules and rituals and strongly traditional. Everyday dealings between adults, too, are full of little courtesies and rituals that we take for granted. An individual's behaviour is strongly influenced by other people's encouragements and expectations about the role he happens to be playing. In these interchanges, individual personality becomes elusive. Perhaps personality is to be understood as a range of competences in social behaviour rather than as a set of fixed qualities.

Our readiness to conspire manifests itself forcefully in our eagerness to identify with a group. Assign an individual, even on the most frivolous grounds, to a group – he need not even know who the other members are – and his behaviour will change. The evidence for that comes from laboratory tests. Real-life studies show that people in groups may alter the way they speak among themselves, to achieve greater vehemence of expression and stronger feelings of intimacy and group identity. Rapid changes of dialect in a modern city may be symptoms of tension developing between opposing groups. Matters of language recur throughout this book, because language is indispensable to so much of our social behaviour.

'Conspiracy' has sinister overtones which are not inappropriate. Our species has long conspired against the wilderness, with big consequences for other species and for the quality of the natural environment. Hunter-gatherers fire the grass to stampede their prey, early farmers abolished the forests of Europe, and modern communities flood whole valleys with their dams. Within our species society breaks up into conspiring groups and our group loyalties become, all too easily, a basis for rivalry and strife.

On the smallest scale we conspire in our face-to-face interactions with other people. We put effort into helping one another to maintain our respective 'fronts' from moment to moment and in doing so dissemble a good deal. Sometimes, too, we cheat and currents of suspicion and mistrust run through social life, from the family circle to national and international affairs. The hallmark of human behaviour is etiquette, rather than love.

Contrasting styles of play. The commonplace observation that young boys play more aggressively than girls do is borne out by a careful review of the scientific evidence.

1 : The Hominid Plot

Any adult watching over a children's party finds that boys make more trouble than the girls do. It is not usually the girls who throw punches or jam tarts, or who prefer wrestling to polite games. Testimony from almost any schoolroom tells the same kind of story. This difference between the sexes, in conduct which has very little to do with the sexual act itself, is the most conspicuous and commonplace example of an effect of biology on human behaviour. Yet to notice it, in the decade of Women's Liberation, is to make a shocking political statement. Regrets on that score may be tempered by the knowledge that the statement is unflattering to the tyrannical sex. It also happens to be correct, according to a most thorough review of the evidence by Eleanor Maccoby and Carol Nagy Jacklin of Stanford University in California.

In one experiment, pairs of two-year-olds are left, in a deliberately provocative situation, with a single toy between them. With two girls, the resulting tussle to grab the toy is usually fairly mild; with two boys, the contest may quickly escalate, as if they were provoking one another in a peculiarly masculine way. When a boy and a girl are left with the toy, the boy is often much less aggressive than he would be towards another boy. Note the qualifying words used here: 'usually', 'often', and so on. Any general statement about how human beings behave must allow for a wide range of individual differences.

Hormones and hemispheres

As it resembles the rough-and-tumble play of young chimpanzees, aggressiveness in young human males is apelike rather than manly. But masculine it certainly is, involving the male sex hormones, which begin to operate even before birth. When mothers have a glandular defect that results in the production of male hormones during pregnancy follow-up studies have shown that their daughters turn out to be 'tomboys'.

The increase in male hormones circulating in the blood of an adolescent male chimpanzee is linked with an upsurge in aggressiveness towards females and other young males. Jane Goodall and Anne Pusey have recently reported from the Gombe Stream Research Centre in Tanzania on these slow and complex changes in behaviour that start in eight-year-old male chimpanzees. Parallel research that relates the adolescent behaviour directly to hormone levels has begun at the spacious primate colony at Stanford. Psychiatrists suspect that the same hormonal surge in both chimpanzee and human male adolescents may give them similar emotional problems.

The boisterousness of boys reflects what I shall call a 'biological bias' in human behaviour. This avoids terms such as 'instinct', 'inborn behaviour' or 'innate tendencies', none of which can be safely used about humans, the least 'instinctive' of animals. A tendency is implied, which derives from the organisation of brain or body and ultimately from the genetic messages of human heredity. But it is not a blind compulsion, just a bias – as in this case. Although small boys expend more energy than girls do, they are not incapable of sitting still. The male sex hormones seem to act directly on the brain, yet there is nothing compulsory about boisterous behaviour in the long run. Learning self-control is an important part of growing to manhood.

The extent to which males or females behave cooperatively or aggressively is strongly influenced by the cultures in which they grow up, and by effects of calming or rousing leadership. A 'cooperation board' devised by Millard Madsen of the University of California, Los Angeles, has been used to study cultural differences. Four children sit around the board, each pulling a string that helps to move a pen. If they

I ignore him...it's merely an apodictive male hormonal surge

cooperate they can guide the pen quite easily to four targets marked on the board, in a sequence, and so win rewards for the group as a whole. In a second phase of the experiment, getting the pen to a particular target wins a reward for one child only. A 'cooperative' group will continue to use the same orderly technique, and go to each target in turn, winning a prize for each child in turn. A 'competitive' group goes wild, with each child aggressively working for himself and nobody succeeding. Children living in cities are more likely to show competitive behaviour than children who have grown up in small rural communities. But in this test situation, where reason may or may not prevail, there is little difference between the sexes.

Adults may reinforce the biological bias by emphasising the norms of male and female behaviour. For example boys are 'meant' to be able to stand up for themselves, while girls observe quite different norms of female behaviour. The female emancipators certainly have a case here. But the social system did not invent the biological bias and anyone conceiving a more just society will be well advised to take it into account, along with differences in how the sexes think about the world.

Girls show greater skill with words than boys do, especially after puberty. Boys run ahead of the girls in visual-spatial tasks – ones that involve complicated shapes or the arrangement of objects in space. Again, individuals vary, but the tests that show their differences have been administered to large numbers of children and adults, so the evidence of overall contrasts between the sexes is secure. Apparently related to the visual-spatial ability of males is a greater precision in throwing, and also markedly greater skill in some kinds of mathematics.

At a time when the human brain's knowledge of its own operations remains sketchy, it might seem hopeless

to look for mechanisms that affect how people answer a riddle or assemble a machine. But these sex differences somehow conform to a major feature of brain organisation. The left side of the brain handles verbal tasks better, while the right side deals more skilfully with visual-spatial tasks. Some scientists make the distinction more general by saying that the left brain is apt to deal with tasks in sequence, whether it be remembering a string of numbers or typing a succession of letters, while the right brain treats objects, symbols or

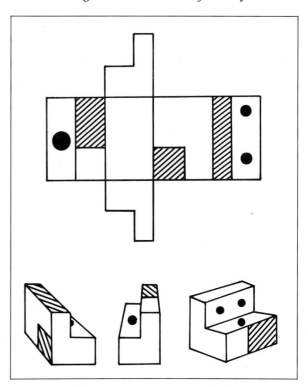

Which of the three folded shapes can be made from the flat shape? In this kind of 'visual-spatial' test men tend to score better than women do. Females on the other hand typically show a greater skill with words. On the right is a page from the manuscript of Daisy Ashford's 'The Young Visiters', written when she was nine.

problems as a whole, and perceives their relationships.

We all have left and right sides to our brains, and can think in either fashion. But the division of labour between the two sides of the brain may be establishing itself sooner in girls than in boys. If girls have a head start in this respect it is not surprising. Boys are late developers, on the whole. The fastest increase in height occurs earlier in girls than in boys (typically at eleven years for girls as against fourteen years for boys). Boys spend longer in the vulnerable periods of childhood

when favourable or unfavourable circumstances can influence their later performance. That may explain both the stupidity and the brilliance that seem to be commoner among males than among females. Girls, however, pay a price for their precocity: language is such a convenient thing, especially in schoolrooms that run on words, that girls tend to apply verbal reasoning to problems, to the neglect of their visual-spatial skills. We should be more on our guard against a verbal bias in the classroom, where most teachers are women.

The reason for raising sex differences in behaviour here is to prepare the way for other biological biases that seem more subtle. As human beings are not creatures of instinct in any crude sense, it is all the harder for us to admit to inherited biases of behaviour that evolved in our human and pre-human ancestors. We have to learn how to behave, but some kinds of learning are much easier for us than others. Just as virtually all human beings learn to walk, so do they learn to speak in their mother tongue. Swimming, on the other hand, requires more study and practice and learning a second language after puberty requires more deliberate effort. Telling other human individuals apart is easy; to distinguish as many different species of flowers may seem harder. These learning preferences are biological biases in our human nature, and they have evolved just as surely as our hands and teeth have evolved.

Comparisons between ourselves and other animals are tricky and sometimes risky, but we can see evolutionary principles at work in their behaviour which may sometimes be relevant to ourselves.

Monkey business

Monkeys, apes and humans are the present-day descendants of mammals that started to live in trees and evolved as primates, very different in their bodies and

brains from other mammals that stayed on terra firma. The treetops offered protection from beasts of prey, but the price was the ever-present risk of falling off, so skill in treework evolved strongly. Evolution proceeds because some animals leave more surviving offspring than others do. They tend to be the ones best suited to their way of life, and their offspring tend to resemble them. More precisely, the more appropriate messages of heredity, or genes, become commoner in the population in succeeding generations. The notion that such natural selection is necessarily a matter of competition and conflict is quite false.

Little by little, typical characteristics of the primates appeared. Although our own ancestors left the trees (or the trees left them) a long time ago, we still share many of those characteristics: grasping hands; powerful and agile arms and legs; eyes that face front on either side of a short nose. The sense of smell became less important among our ancestral primates, but brains grew larger, bringing quick-wittedness. There were social developments, too. Young primates took an increasingly long time to reach maturity, so protection of the young and their mothers became an important factor. Monkeys and apes invested an increasing amount of brain power and daily effort in trying to manage their social relationships.

The typical primate today needs very little of his intelligence to gather his food. He carefully watches the behaviour of the others in his troop, and shows measured control of his own emotions. The fierceness that a male monkey may display against a strange intruder is moderated in a confrontation with a subordinate male of his own group and is greatly restrained toward an annoying infant. No fierceness is shown in the presence of a dominant male, even if the dominant male is antagonistic.

The baboons of the African savanna provide some striking examples of primate behaviour. These animals are interesting because, like early man, they live, vulnerably, in open country. When moving across dangerous terrain, a troop of baboons adopts a characteristic formation. Irven DeVore of Harvard University describes it like this: 'The females and young keep near to the dominant males in the centre. Other males are at the rear of the group and in front. Suppose a leopard, with a taste for baboon meat, blocks their path. Reacting to a warning bark, the males boldly mass to face and rout the leopard, while the females and youngsters run for their lives. Baboons whose genes encourage such co-operative behaviour against a predator will survive more often and leave more offspring with the same genes and behaviour. Under these conditions a solitary baboon is soon a dead baboon.'

Each baboon knows exactly where he stands in the hierarchy of the troop, but existing dominant males are always liable to challenge by younger males. In old age, dominant males avoid unnecessary contests and may, for example, defer to younger males in disputes over food; yet they still assert themselves when females are fertile. Although an old hungry philandering baboon can have no conception of evolutionary principles, evolution has sorted out for him his order of priorities as between food and sex.

Yet the baboons are not acting by mere reflexes: they are intelligent animals that adapt their behaviour to suit the conditions; and this adaptability, too, is part of what their evolution has given them. When experimenters have transferred an individual baboon into a troop of a different species, with quite different habits, they are amazed at how quickly the newcomer learns to conform. In their social organisation baboons are quite advanced, but they are not as closely related to human beings as gorillas and chimpanzees.

Among chimpanzees, life is more relaxed. They are

unconcerned about predators or defending a territory and a dominant male is much less aggressive than a boss baboon. A chimpanzee may sit cheerfully by while a junior male copulates with a favoured female. Evolution seems to have taken promiscuity in the female chimpanzee for granted. As a result the males have evolved giant testicles as if outbidding one another in the production of sperm and so promoting each individual's chances of fatherhood.

Intellectual stimulation seems to have its own rewards for a chimpanzee. A Canadian psychologist was one day encouraging a captive female to solve problems by awarding her slices of banana, but he ran out of bananas. Thereupon the chimpanzee turned to a stock of banana slices that she had accumulated and returned them to the experimenter so that the game could continue. These other primates show us baselines of behavioural competence below which we are not likely to have fallen. We can hardly be less adaptable to changing circumstances than baboons are, nor less interested in puzzles and games than a chimpanzee.

In many respects we humans, with our sharp eyes, big brains, clever hands and social sensibility continue the traditions of monkeys and apes. But mark also how we have changed. Beside apparent trivialities like our loss of hair and increased sweatiness, important marks of our humanity include our upright posture, striding gait and hands capable of precise work. The differences between men and women, in both stature and behaviour, are much less marked than the differences between male and female apes. An intense and continuous sex life makes the human being an uncommon animal. Our bodily chemistry has committed us to eating at least some animal food, to obtain, in particular, vitamin B_{12}. We are cleverer than the apes, and more emotional too, yet better able to conceal and manage our emotions. Apes use simple tools, but we make tools of a quite dif-

ferent order and have become wholly dependent on them. Our special gift of spoken language is another distinguishing mark which goes with a capacity for social organisation far surpassing that of apes.

Playing at being Bushmen

Our early human ancestors passed through a long phase of gathering wild plants and hunting wild animals. Even after people just like ourselves, *Homo sapiens sapiens*, appeared on the planet about 50,000 years ago, they continued the old way of life. The invention of agriculture some 10,000 years ago drastically changed it, but farming and the settled civilisations it brought in its wake have taken all of the intervening time to commandeer the world. The few tribes of hunter-gatherers that have survived into the twentieth century give us some impression of the life to which the biology and behaviour of our species were first suited before farming took the natural sport out of our lives. But only an impression. No one can be sure that the ancestors of present-day farmers and manufacturers followed any of the social conventions of present-day hunter-gatherers.

In the nick of time, anthropologists and film-makers have recorded the traditional way of life of the Bushmen. These dignified and egalitarian people have lived by hunting and gathering, ranging freely in the semi-desert of southern Africa. The Bushmen used to say 'Why should we plant crops when there are so many mongongo nuts in the world?' But today they are being resettled in farming communities. Their new life conforms to the conventional notions of progress, but their traditional way of life is certainly not wretched.

In the hot, dry climate they need to rest a lot; they can afford to do so, because they can usually collect ample food to keep everyone well nourished and healthy, in quite a short time. Youngsters and old people are not expected to 'work' at all. But water is scarce and the Bushmen have to move repeatedly from waterhole to waterhole. They travel light. Their equipment for hunting, generally regarded as the men's responsibility, includes bows and poisoned arrows. For gathering plant foods, seen primarily as the women's task, the tools consist of digging sticks, nutcracking stones and skin containers.

The Bushmen are eloquent storytellers. They have music and sometimes will dance all night. In their heads is encyclopaedic knowledge of the topography of all the places they have visited, the plant life and the game. And they know the tricks of hunting, for instance, that burning the land can attract game by releasing water from the roots of plants.

The women are lean and well-exercised, and they breastfeed their babies until they are three or four years old. That prevents ovulation, menstruation and pregnancy, and as a result they normally have babies every four years, which keeps the population in balance from generation to generation. There is the very occasional, grief-laden, resort to infanticide if a baby comes 'too early'. Judging by the Bushmen, frequent menstruation may indeed be a 'curse', that came to women only when they settled in farms and cities. Among the Bushmen in the new settlements, babies are weaned younger, the population is exploding, and the status of women has declined.

For the first year at least the mother in a traditional Bushman group carries her baby wherever she goes, slung at her side. Even the smallest baby is able to cling effectively, using grasps and reflexes that seem meaningless in a baby in a modern cot, and he is allowed to feed at any time he wants to. Young Bushmen grow up in a tightly-knit society of adults and children, where they are free to observe the events of adult life, and all

Gatherers and hunters of southern Africa. These Bushmen are carrying palm-heart on their hunting expedition.

teaching takes the form of participation by the child in adult activities. In their games older children play at being gatherers or hunters or hunted animals. A great deal of play involves both adults and children.

The culture of the wandering Bushmen has shown a durability unmatched by any elaborate civilisation. They have been following the same sort of life in the same area for at least 11,000 years. Have they had a secret recipe for social survival? Here, for the reader to judge, are some features of recent Bushman society. They live in temporary encampments of around thirty-five people, related by 'blood' and marriage. These Bushman families wander over huge areas and re-groupings occur to suit the changing degrees of drought. Territory means little to them. Sometimes several families will camp together and cooperate for a while before going their different ways. The family groups typically centre on a core of brothers and sisters – thus neatly disposing of recent sex-chauvinist theories that claim either patriarchy or matriarchy to be the 'natural' line of authority among humans.

Before a man can marry he has to prove his skill in hunting and ritual, and then he is expected to go and live with his wife's people, at least for some years. If he marries a 'central' woman he may become a leading figure in her group. But leadership is a modest word among the Bushmen: decisions are reached by consensus among both men and women. Even in risky conditions, they may spend days deciding that it is high time to move to the next waterhole. If serious disputes develop within a family group it simply splits up – a remedy not available to more encumbered and settled societies.

An ingenious piece of social engineering is the assumption that two Bushmen who have the same name are related. They may not be, but the convention has the effect of making sure that the available food is shared widely. Adult Bushmen spend a good deal of time on friendly visits to neighbouring groups.

The triumph of sociability and the possibility of widespread kindliness, well represented in the Bushmen, are the most puzzling of the many remarkable things that occurred in the leap from apes to humans. As we shall see, much of the recent writing and talk about our human aggressiveness has been wide of the mark. Even if it were not, biologists have never had any difficulty in seeing why aggressiveness and other forms of selfish behaviour may evolve in almost any species including our own. But the moderation of aggressiveness, the control of selfishness, the establishment of norms of mutual assistance – these qualities of human life are much harder to explain in evolutionary terms.

The very concept of evolution derives from comparisons between animals. Already baboons and Bushmen have figured in this account and, as we move on to other species and to speculation about our most primitive forebears, the reader may well wonder about their relevance to our human concerns in the twentieth century. Keep in mind that the achievements and faults of our present civilisation derive from long-lasting patterns of behaviour and the intrinsic quality of life on Earth.

With his treatise *Sociobiology*, published in 1975, E. O. Wilson of Harvard University sought to put the biological approach to social behaviour on a firm and broad footing. Much of his scholarly and original book deals in loving detail with the social life of birds, bees and other beasts. As for human beings, Wilson says, 'history, biography and fiction are the research protocols of human ethology, and anthropology and sociology together constitute the sociobiology of a single primate species'. But he is at pains to emphasise the peculiarities of human social behaviour. Indeed, he sees in human societies the reversal of a long-running trend in evolution, which has led other animals away from cohesion and cooperation.

Some of the older and more primitive kinds of animals, such as corals, produce almost perfect societies, in which each member is so fully a part of it that the colony is like a single superorganism. The next pinnacle of social evolution comes with the social insects – ants, termites, wasps and bees. They are remarkable for their elaborate organisation and the self-sacrifice of individuals, but there are conflicts of interest about the right to breed, which may be exclusively arrogated by a single queen. Among the animals with backbones, though, cooperation is often rudimentary and selfishness rules the relationships between members of a social group.

'By human standards, life in a fish school or a baboon troop is tense and brutal,' Wilson remarks. Some intelligent mammals work at being sociable, among them lions, hunting dogs, monkeys and apes. They are able to exploit their abilities of recognition, of signalling, of learning and of modulating their responses towards their colleagues. But the interests of individuals and cliques limit the degree to which the typical vertebrate society can act as a unit. For Wilson the culminating mystery of all biology is how humans alone have been able to transcend these difficulties of vertebrate life in achieving an extraordinary degree of cooperation at a new pinnacle in social evolution.

Two main theories are now on offer to account for it. One of them sees some similarities in principle between the ants on the one hand and the families and tribes of early man on the other. Apart from explaining group cooperation, its conclusions about human propensities are unflattering. Another theory, as we shall see, is more optimistic about the evolutionary tendencies that underlie human cooperation. As both may well be valid in part, I shall describe the two theories, before going on to see which of them the evidence may favour. We start with a digression into the world of ants, but the analogies with human behaviour are not far behind.

Love thy sister

Ants provide a fascinating parody of human social life. Living in cities of thousands or millions of individuals, they are organised into social castes of soldiers, outdoor workers and indoor workers – all female, all serving a queen. The males are selfish, contributing nothing to the colony until the time comes for the mating flights. A foraging column of ants is formidable. If they encounter ants from a rival colony messages go back to call out the troops, and a battle ensues between the soldiers that leaves the field strewn with little corpses – lives laid down for queen and colony.

When one also knows that some species of ants grow their food in gardens and others keep aphids for milking, the drawing of parallels between ants and humans becomes a temptation indeed – and some social commentators have failed to resist it. Biologists have been more sceptical. Impressive though they are, ants are not at all like us. Their totalitarian societies are mindlessly governed by exchanges of chemical signals between pin-brained animals.

Yet ants are more like humans than even chimpanzees are, in the extraordinary degree to which they act for the benefit of other ants rather than for their own self-interest – in other words, their altruism. The contrast between altruism and selfishness is the distinction in social behaviour, as perceived by biologists, that corresponds most closely to the human contrast between right and wrong. Selfishness in the biological sense is almost self-explanatory, although it does include care of one's own offspring. Altruistic behaviour means benefiting another individual at some cost to oneself.

Collaboration among ants. Some individual army ants have formed a bridge with their bodies, while others struggle across it with the captured young of another ant species. Ants have achieved highly cooperative societies, but on a different principle from humans.

The question of how altruism, and the kindliness and cooperation that flow from it, could possibly evolve among animals puzzled Charles Darwin himself. On any simple view, the bully, the cheat or the cannibal ought to prosper. By securing more mates or more food or the safest home, the selfish animal would ensure that he left plenty of surviving offspring, with the same selfish characteristics, while any cooperative, unselfish animal would suffer and his line would quickly die out. Plainly something else has happened because in some animals, including ants and humans, highly cooperative behaviour has become almost the norm. The worker ants leave no offspring at all, so how can their habits of service to the colony be transmitted to later generations? No offspring, no behaviour!

Darwin feared that the ants might annihilate his whole theory, until he reasoned that the members of a colony form a single family. Natural selection could therefore be applied to the family as a whole as well as to individuals. But biologists were slow to develop this notion of evolution by families, or to pursue the problem of altruism, although the leading geneticists, J. B. S. Haldane and R. A. Fisher, considered them. Only in the 1960s did issues of altruism come to the fore again. Some investigators have striven to see how natural selection working on individuals could generate some of its features. A wolf, for instance, that is either too aggressive or too submissive in fights with other wolves may have less chance of perpetuating his genes than one which is peaceable but fights back when necessary. William Hamilton of Imperial College, London, on the other hand, began modernising Darwin's notion of selection acting on families.

The essence of the theory is that genes favouring altruistic actions can be passed on to new generations by near-relatives of the altruistic individuals. Provided the benefit to the genes transmitted via the relatives exceeds the cost to the genes transmitted by the altruistic individuals, altruistic behaviour can evolve. In Hamilton's terminology, the 'inclusive fitness', which considers the individual and his relatives together, can be assessed in natural selection.

The worker ants are sisters of the queen. If a sterile worker possesses the right genes for unselfish behaviour, the queen may carry them too, not making use of them herself but passing them to the next generation of workers. If her fertile offspring have a better chance of surviving and breeding because of the altruistic behaviour of the workers, then the genes will survive and the behaviour can evolve, consolidating itself in the life of ants. To prove that this is what really happened during ant evolution is not easy, but an extension of Hamilton's theory has led to a remarkable prediction. It involves another aspect of ant behaviour.

Even if the queen ant lays all the eggs, the worker ants regulate the population of the colony by destroying surplus young. Now, in their infanticide they distinguish between males and females. Because of a peculiarity of the sex life of ants, a worker has three times as many of her genes in common with the female young as she has in common with the male young. If she lets too many males survive she will be putting too much work into supporting lazy males genetically different from herself. If, on the other hand, she kills too many males, she will give the genes of the remaining males a big advantage over her own genes, by increasing the survivors' mating opportunities. Robert Trivers of Harvard University reasoned that a worker would be well advised, for the best perpetuation of her own genes, to devote three times as much effort to maintaining her sisters as to her brothers. This prediction is made by no other theory and it can be checked by weighing the ants of the two sexes – weight being a measure of invested resources. Trivers finds that in

I know I'm a Mummy's boy ....but am I Daddy's?

many ant colonies, where there are no other factors at work, the weight of all the female ants is almost exactly three times the weight of all the males. Unthinkingly, guided by genes that shape their behaviour, the worker ants act in such a way as to fulfil the ruthless arithmetic of gene survival.

Any carry-over from ants to humans of notions about the evolution of behaviour is bound to be provocative. But at least one feature of human behaviour has, for the biologist, an uncanny equivalence with the altruism of the worker ant. It is homosexuality. Leaving aside all contentious issues about the mechanisms that might produce homosexuality, what is in question is why evolution should allow the survival of genes that permit homosexuality to develop. On the simplest view of evolution, heterosexuals leave notably more surviving offspring than homosexuals do, so any tendency to homosexuality should simply die out and the very possibility of such behaviour should be extinguished. Yet a substantial minority of humans are homosexual and many of them produce no children at all. Presumably, like the worker ants, they serve their communities and relatives. If their work so benefits their near-relatives as to increase the relatives' chances of survival and reproduction, the genes that allow for the possibility of homosexuality can survive with them.

Feuding families

The benefits of living altruistically with one's family provide one mechanism whereby the cooperative behaviour of human beings might have begun. The zoologist J. Z. Young suggests that the mass production of genetically identical people might serve as a technical means for improving altruism among humans of the future. It would certainly make us more ant-like! But other kinds of behaviour besides altruism can evolve through the same mechanism of the family genes. At this point, the attempts to bring human social behaviour within the purview of the evolutionary biology of families evoke unpleasant possibilities.

For instance Robert Trivers, already mentioned as one whose work is complementary to William Hamilton's, has looked behind the curtains at tensions of domestic life. He regards some of them as consequences of evolutionary realities that centre on the large investment of time and effort that humans and some other animals put into rearing their young. It is in the parent's interest to be free of caring for a child (perhaps to rear other children) while the child's interest lies in sponging on his parents for as long as possible. Older infants revert to babyish behaviour to demand more maternal attention. Meanwhile parents will attempt to make a reluctant child be kind to his aunts and cousins, who are more closely related to the parents than they are to the child.

Between the mother and father there exists the possibility that one or other will desert in the midst of the child-rearing process. By heartless calculation of the genetic pay-off, it may well suit the less committed parent (usually the male) to go off and breed further with someone else provided the survival of the first children is not unduly jeopardised. The niceties and hesitations of human courtship seem to reflect a search for guarantees against desertion or other forms of ill-treatment.

The notoriously unfair 'double standard' that winks at male infidelity but sees female infidelity as a scandalous or even murderous matter also makes perfect sense biologically. A woman can be sure that any child she bears carries half her genes. A man can never be quite certain that a child is his and a measure of jealousy and suspicion helps to protect him against spending years of his life unwittingly rearing children who carry none

27

Family politics. By intermarriage, royalty traditionally tried to exploit the altruism of the family tribe in international affairs — not always with conspicuous success. Queen Victoria (centre of the upper photograph) had a large family scattered through Europe. Nevertheless her grandsons George V (seated, centre, in the lower photograph) and Wilhelm II (standing behind George V) confronted each other in the First World War.

Egyptian battle-scene. Theories that emphasise family genetics within tribes could make warfare a natural consequence of the evolution of human altruism.

of his own genes. Men too vulnerable to cuckolding will tend to disappear by natural selection, but it should be mentioned that they will include men lacking in love as well as those deficient in jealousy.

William Hamilton takes a decidedly pessimistic view of what evolution by families may have implanted in human nature. In both ants and humans, warfare and slavery have coexisted with strong altruistic bonds within the local group. In his most recent theorising, Hamilton envisages strong effects of tribalism during human evolution. The mathematical notion of 'inclusive fitness' copes particularly well with fuzzy 'blood' relationships within and between neighbouring tribes.

The theory predicts that the level which altruism can reach within a tribe is limited by migrations between tribes. If a tribe has no immigrants, inbreeding makes the members more highly related to one another – more and more like an ant colony – giving increasing scope for a natural family communism in which altruism pays off through its benefits to one's own genes carried by relatives. Ill-effects of inbreeding, though, make immigration desirable in principle, while emigration is, in evolutionary terms, a way of increasing the success of one's own genes by spreading them far and wide. Immigrants might, though, dilute the altruism within a tribe, unless they are themselves good altruists, so Hamilton would expect a probationary period during which immigrants might be treated with hostility and suspicion.

Migrations help to reduce genetic contrasts between tribes but, except in unusual circumstances, Hamilton imagines a sharp drop in relatedness from one tribe to the next. It might therefore be advantageous to the propagation of one's genes – including those favouring altruism within the tribe – to wage war and acquire land, women, slaves and material goods. Although evolution does not necessarily avoid a harmful tendency, Hamilton contests the commonplace view that warfare is self-evidently harmful from the point of view of the species. Many living species, including our own, have prospered in spite of warfare and other wasteful activities. But whatever natural selection may have said about warfare in the past, Hamilton observes, today's frightful armaments do endanger the survival of our species.

Deceit, cruelty, terror and torture also fit into his picture, and he regards the relatively peaceful Bushmen as exceptional. All in all, Hamilton says, 'the animal in our nature cannot be regarded as a fit custodian for the values of civilised man'. He is one of the few scientists of distinction who quotes with approval the writings of Robert Ardrey, the best-selling depictor of the beast in man. And some readers may accept all this reasoning as a licence to shrug one's shoulders about war, racism and genocide. Hamilton's own view is that we are concerned in humans with 'amorphous and variable inclinations' rather than with instincts, but that only by knowing how deep-rooted in our nature some of the more lamentable inclinations may be can we adequately organise the world to keep them in check.

A third and real possibility is that the diagnosis is incorrect. It might be false because all genetic logic of this kind is for some reason inappropriate to the evolution of human beings. Or Hamilton may have the wrong picture of what was going on among our ancestors. While Hamilton emphasises the importance of family and tribal relationships in human evolution, Robert Trivers describes an evolutionary escape route into cooperation between non-relatives. As a shift in emphasis it is like the transition from the Old Testament to the New Testament. But the love for neighbours that emerges from his theory is not pure and unstinted.

Human altruism. British blood donors are not paid, but they volunteer in large numbers. Making a direct sacrifice for the benefit of non-relatives is almost unique to humans and the evolutionary riddle that it poses is only now being solved.

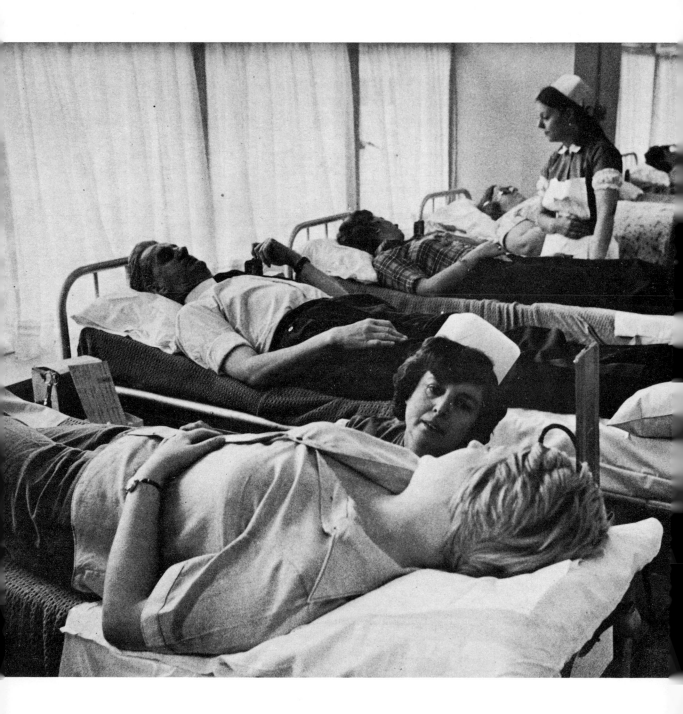

Give and take

A man is apparently drowning and I see his peril. By world-wide norms of human behaviour I have to jump in the water and try to save him, provided I am fit and a competent swimmer and have a reasonable chance of success. But why is that the expected thing to do? After all, there is no shortage of people in the world.

Any issue of life and death, such as the drowning man poses, is of great theoretical interest to biologists, because survival and the failure to survive are the very stuff of evolution. Suppose there is a considerable chance of the victim perishing if I do not rescue him, and a small but not zero chance of my dying in the cold water if I make the attempt. If the man were a near relative, a brother say, he would be carrying many of my own genes. Then the arithmetic of risk would clearly imply more benefit to my genes from helping him than not helping him.

Seeing that the man is no relative, I have to bring a different kind of reasoning into play. I can well put my genes at risk to save him if I think that one day I may be out there drowning, and he or one of his friends will save me – or perhaps save a child of mine. Then my genes will benefit in the long run from the present risk I take by jumping in. That is the principle of give-and-take, or reciprocal altruism. It is a cooperative principle that plainly operates in human affairs, extending far beyond life-saving situations. The principle could be invented by reason and sustained by training. But it also turns out to be workable in a more biological fashion. If it actually benefits the genes, the behaviour is capable of evolving.

Robert Trivers launched the theory in 1971, in a paper just twenty pages long called *The Evolution of Reciprocal Altruism*. In some respects it is similar to Hamilton's theories about family genes, the all-impor-

tant difference being that it is not confined to relatives. It extends across all the wider associations of human society and the cooperation between non-relatives that is conspicuous. Trivers finds 'inclusive fitness' enhanced by acts of assistance and kindness, given and received. So evolution could, in effect, build this norm of good behaviour into us. It does not make us entirely saintly, because people can cheat.

The theory suggests that our sense of right and wrong is built into us among our biological biases. Curiously this idea strikes some people as more repellent than the frequent propositions that man's aggressiveness and wickedness are parts of his animal nature. Yet even that reaction might be interpreted as part of the evolutionary programme, if the learned explanation interferes with the virtuous feelings that people experience when they have performed a good deed.

A simple game for two players sums up much of the uncertainty and tension of human social life. It is called the Prisoner's Dilemma, and is well known to game theorists, psychologists and now evolutionists. The game is so arranged that if each person plays selfishly, villain against villain, both players lose and go on systematically losing. If the players tacitly agree to cooperate, saint and saint, both of them will win systematically, but slowly. The big prizes come to the cheat who fools the other player into thinking he is a saint and suddenly turns villain. A saint playing against a villain loses heavily and becomes a sucker.

But the defector then becomes liable to retaliation and he can find himself locked into a villain versus villain situation which before long wipes out his gains. Unless both players are willing to risk being suckers – to play the saint often and offer cooperation – they are both bound to lose. So the players have to keep probing and testing each other's behaviour, warily offering saintly trust in return for trust. Their choice of 'moves'

A game beyond pure reason

The story behind the game of the Prisoner's Dilemma is of an interrogator separately questioning two men guilty of a serious crime. He has evidence to convict them both of a lesser crime even if neither confesses, but he can 'nail' them for the more serious offence only with a confession. If both confess, they will both receive less than the maximum sentence. If one confesses and the other does not the confessor will go scot-free while the other will suffer the maximum penalty.

The prisoners cannot consult together and each is in a real dilemma because he does not know what the other will do. Prisoner A's best result comes if he confesses while Prisoner B does not. But if B also confesses, hoping for this selfish outcome, then they both go down for faily long sentences. If A denies the charge and B does the same, they will both fare reasonably well, suffering only a short sentence for the lesser crime. But if A denies the charge, while B confesses, then A becomes the sucker who receives the maximum sentence while the other goes free.

To generalise the game, call a denial of the charge a 'saintly' move and a confession a 'villainous' move – broader questions of legality and honesty being irrelevant. Then assign scores as follows:

> *A plays the saint*
> if B is saintly, A and B both score 1
> if B is villainous, A loses 10, B wins 10
>
> *A plays the villain*
> if B is saintly, A scores 10, B loses 10
> if B is villainous, A and B both lose 1

Logic might prescribe villainy as the best strategy, but the outcome if both follow it is unsatisfactory. The best result for the two prisoners taken together comes from saintliness by both. But for either of them to decide upon it independently is hazardous and involves issues of motive, trust and personality concerning the other prisoner.

in the game is equivalent to cooperating or cheating in an altruistic society. Trivers suggests that evolution has schooled us in such a game.

In life as in the Prisoner's Dilemma, saintliness pays off only if the other players are not villains. But anyone is liable to cheat a little when he thinks he can get away with it. Evolution may have taken account of this danger to the basis of human cooperation, of the saint proving to be a sucker, by biasing each of us to hate a cheat (other than oneself) and to have an acute sense of fairness and justice. Trivers illustrates this proposition by the disproportionate sense of outrage that may be felt and expressed in a line of people waiting to be served at a counter, when someone breaks in ahead. The indignation is in fact more unpleasant and costly to the individuals showing it, than having to wait a few moments longer. Such behaviour would be biologically unsuitable, in fact, unless it had evolved for a more serious purpose.

According to Trivers, evolution has tuned our emotions and our judgements of other people to the needs of the system of give-and-take. We like another person who seems to be unselfish and trustworthy, but the driving emotions of sympathy and gratitude involve calculations about the plight and the remedy. And as humans are very adept at feigning friendship or sympathy, or pretending to be in need of help, a capacity for suspiciousness may also have evolved. For the cheat, the price of being found out may be very high. So Trivers reasons that the feeling of guilt is yet another mechanism that has evolved as part of the package of give-and-take.

All these aspects of behaviour are explained rather easily as what you would expect evolution to build into an animal that relies heavily on reciprocal altruism and is also clever enough to cheat. Humans are by far the best qualified species in both respects. There are continual tensions between direct selfishness and the enlightened self interest of reciprocal altruism. And selfishness and altruism between non-relatives are of a different character from those inside the family. They usually involve cooler emotions.

Social scientists find Trivers' theory unpalatable. Reciprocal altruism is 'old hat' as far as sociological theory is concerned. All the mechanisms and checks and feelings might be just the same if they were learnt rather than inherited. Altruistic behaviour could be simply a by-product of massive brain-power, as music might be thought to be. Or it could come from the special aptitude of human beings to learn the rules and norms of their society. In any case an emphasis on give-and-take is, some say, part of the 'sociology of the good guys' that reflects the ideology of Protestant America.

As no way of testing the Trivers theory seems to be available at present, such criticisms cannot be dismissed out of hand. But the social scientists may not fully sense the strength of the evolutionary tide that flows against cooperation between animals that are not relatives. The disruptive effects of competition for mates, and the near-certainty that an altruistic animal will be a sucker unless the others are altruistic too, tend automatically to suppress cooperation and to eliminate genes that even permit it. In evolution theory, it really does not matter what the mechanism is, that offers altruistic behaviour. It could be a feeling of satisfaction from helping someone else; or spare brain capacity that allows one to work out the benefits of cooperation and give-and-take; or merely a special readiness to learn the rules and behave as others say you should behave. Whatever the mechanism, it is in danger of being overwhelmed and 'evolved out' by the short-term advantages of selfishness. The difference between altruism and music in this respect is that music does not put

your genes at hazard, unless your performance is singularly discordant.

That is why I have set out the contrasting ideas of William Hamilton and Robert Trivers about the evolution of altruism, expecting also that the biological underpinning of human cooperation will give us a better sense of what kind of animals we are. Assuming that Hamilton's picture of devoted but feuding families and Trivers' more optimistic account of give-and-take between non-relatives are the only ones available, can we find evidence favouring one or the other?

Climates for ancestors

The record of our early human parentage is extremely sketchy so far. Through the period when our ancestors first separated from the ancestors of the chimpanzee and gorilla, there is a gap of millions of years. During that time, rainfall in East Africa was diminishing, because Antarctica was gathering ice and cooling the world. It is widely supposed that the resulting thinning of the forest forced our ape-like ancestors out from the trees, into the grassland, and up on their legs.

By three million years ago, at least two kinds of hominids – animals classified as men – coexisted in East Africa. One was *Australopithecus,* who was about four feet tall and with a brain about the size of a gorilla's, or less than 40 per cent of a typical modern human's. His legs did not permit a striding gait like ours; he must have trotted, not walked. For a while, though, *Australopithecus* seemed a strong candidate to be a direct ancestor of ours, until the discovery of the remains of other hominids, designated *Homo* sp., who lived in East Africa at the same time, with bigger brains and with skulls and leg-bones more like those of present-day men. These hominids made tools such as pebble-choppers and hand-axes and their hunting and

scavenging way of life is attested by the animal scraps found in their living places.

By a million years ago, *Homo erectus* was strutting about, almost as tall as ourselves and with an average brain size about three-quarters of ours. He lived in Africa, Europe, China, and other parts of the world, and he had fire. We glimpse some of his hunting skills at a Spanish site where elephants seem to have been driven by fire into a swamp and there killed.

Humans now classed by the fossil-hunters as *Homo sapiens*, but not yet fully like ourselves, began to show up around a quarter of a million years ago, and by somewhat more than a hundred thousand years ago they included Neanderthal man, who may be reckoned our immediate predecessor. Neanderthal man was not nearly as ungainly as many people imagine – he has been thoroughly libelled on the basis of a diseased skeleton. Vast numbers of Neanderthal tools of many different types are known, varying from locality to locality. And evidence of a degree of 'spiritual' life comes from ceremonial burials of dead Neanderthalers, along with implements, food and flowers; also from cave-bear skulls arranged symbolically in a cave, as if they were objects of veneration.

Some skulls found in the Middle East seem to be intermediate between Neanderthalers and modern man. And genetic comparisons among present-day human populations fit very well with the theory that modern humans appeared in one place – the Middle East – and then gradually spread all over the world, changing their skin colours and other features to suit the environments in which they found themselves living.

With the transition to the modern form, mankind took off. The ancestors' careers had been undistinguished: they were clever and unusual animals but their numbers probably remained small and while they outwitted the animals among whom they moved, they scarcely rose above them. *Homo sapiens sapiens* had altogether more style, evident in his art, his craftsmanship and his rapidly growing inventiveness. He crossed open water, which the Neanderthalers had feared to do. In due course he invented agriculture and settled down. Quite soon afterwards, on the geological timescale, he was flying to the Moon.

Big gaps in the record of early human evolution prevent us from knowing where, how or why the successive species of hominids first appeared. And the fossil remains say very little about social organisation and behaviour. The fossil-hunters cannot be sure of the numbers in typical early human groups, or what kind of interaction there was between adjacent groups. About subtler matters, like the development of human powers of speech, or marital relationships, the bones are entirely mute.

We know more about the circumstances. Three million years ago East Africa was better watered than it is today. About two million years ago a rapid succession of ice ages began. Massive ice sheets smothered huge areas of the northern continents but brief respites, warmer intervals like the one we live in now, have occurred many times. Everywhere our human ancestors wandered, and even in the homeland of tropical Africa, frequent and drastic changes of climate – between warmth and cold, floods and droughts – dogged them, repeatedly wiping out or displacing resources on which they depended. It was a harsh schooling, but it made human beings evolve much more quickly than they might otherwise have done. The size of the brain doubled in three million years.

Don't love thy sister

Picture the formerly lush grassland of East Africa, with its abundance of animals, big and small, and among

Contest of scavengers. On the East African grassland a party of the earliest true men, short and small-brained by our standards, has come upon a great carcase. In this reconstruction by Sarah Landry (made in consultation with Clark Howell) the men cooperate in driving off the hyenas and sabretooth cats.

them groups of our hominid ancestors possessing adult brains the size of a present-day one-year-old child. What was going on between themselves, as parties looked around for fruit and nuts, or dextrously snatched up meat, or followed the honeyguide bird to the bees' nest? What blend of affection and tension existed between them, as they assembled at night, listening to beasts howling in the darkness and colleagues making love? When one hominid family encountered another at a waterhole did they greet each other with smiles and embraces, or snarls and blows? In short, what kind of plot were they hatching?

The word 'plot' hints at a measure of deliberate behaviour, a joint exercise of choice, and that is not carelessness on my part. We take it for granted that today people acting collectively can make societies of many different kinds, from the little warring cannibal tribes of the New Guinea highlands, to a unified communist state the size of China. At some stage in our evolution, the sense of options must have begun to take effect, with hominids preferring one kind of behaviour to another. A leading geneticist, C. H. Waddington of Edinburgh, considered that students of the evolution of behaviour always paid too little attention to the exercise of options. A philosophical minefield sprawls across the savanna here, with awkward concepts like 'free will' and 'consciousness' ready to blow up under one's feet. Let us skirt it, merely holding to the notion that, to some degree, our ancestors will have been aware of the implications and cost-effectiveness of alternative courses of social action.

Hastening onwards to safer ground, we come upon a contrary case, where biology pre-empts human choice. The prohibition of incest is often acclaimed as a human invention, distinguishing us from the reckless beasts but requiring religious or legal enforcement. To some anthropologists, the incest taboo is the cornerstone of human society. That may well be so, but it turns out to involve a very pronounced biological bias, at least in the prevention of brother-sister mating. There ought to be no surprise about it.

The prime benefit of the prohibition of incest is unmistakably biological; by preventing inbreeding it avoids the accumulation of harmful mutant genes in a family line. If behaviour has direct biological consequences we must expect evolution to deal with it, and to discourage incest in species that might be harmed by it. There have been plenty of recent hints of incest-avoiding behaviour, in rodents and in other primates. In 1975, a report from the Gombe Stream Research Centre told of the social mechanism for avoiding inbreeding among the baboons thereabouts.

All male baboons transfer out of the troop into which they were born. From 1967 to 1975, the observers in Tanzania kept careful tabs on the membership of two or three baboon troops, out of seven troops in the vicinity of the research station. None of the twenty males who attained adulthood during this period remained in their parental troop: two disappeared, three died and fifteen changed troops. The transfers occur at between six and eight years of age, just when the male baboons are achieving their full size. Those who are slow to leave may achieve a temporary importance among the males of their original troop, but they have very little to do with the fertile females and in the end they go.

Lions have a similar system. Observers in the Serengeti National Park (also in Tanzania) find that the core of each pride of lions is a group of closely related females. Males leave the pride into which they were born, at the age of about three. They wander around in small groups, on the lookout for prides where the resident males, ageing or few in number, can be driven out and condemned to a solitary existence. The baboons are not so callous about ageing males and young males joining a new troop have to work to establish their place in it.

New evidence of a biological bias against brother-sister incest in humans is even more remarkable. Evolution has made quite a sure thing of this taboo. The brain of a child evidently photographs, as it were, all children of the opposite sex with whom he or she is living *en famille* and thereafter will never have serious sexual relations with them. This negative 'imprinting' compares and contrasts with the process by which a newly hatched bird falls in love with the first moving object it sees, hopefully its mother. In humans the critical period seems to be between birth and six years of age. The evidence comes where children grow up together with no legal or biological barrier to later marriage, as among the unrelated youngsters who lead the communal life of an Israeli kibbutz. By sheer opportunity many marriages, or at least affairs, would be expected between such children when they grow up. Yet they simply do not occur, as a thorough check of large numbers of individuals has shown.

Leocidal lions

The evidence from Israel about present-day humans, and the analogies from the primates, suggest that outbreeding was going on, too, among our early ancestors. An evolved aversion from incest, already working in the hominids, would have implications for other behaviour and for the genetics of altruism. We have to imagine the young hominid adults, displaced from their families, striving diffidently or heartily to make friends with a family or group other than their own, winning a mate there and proving their worth with gifts and deeds beneficial to the group.

Aversion from incest favours an emphasis on altruism between non-relatives, as described by Trivers. It is not a conclusive argument, because one could imagine the youngsters forever shuttling to and fro between a pair of family groups, mating with their cousins, to preserve the family ties described by Hamilton. But other pieces of evidence point to behaviour of the Trivers sort as the main ingredient of the hominid plot. One is the cooperation between non-relatives that is commonplace in human social behaviour today. Another is the human reversal of animal tendencies to murder.

In the 1960s the critics hailed Konrad Lorenz's *On Aggression* as 'one of the most important books of our age'. The judgement was premature. Lorenz argued that man's killer instinct is less controlled than in the most savage of animals. He noted the ritualised behaviour and inhibitions that often operate to prevent fights between two animals of the same species leading to serious injury or death. It is particularly striking in predatory animals armed with sharp teeth and claws, which could easily do one another great damage. Among such animals, Lorenz reasoned, the inhibitions against killing one another had to be strongest and most reliable. Alas, he went on, our human ancestors did not need such inhibitory mechanisms preventing sudden manslaughter because without weapons humans were basically harmless. Then, when artificial weapons came into a man's hands, you had Cain striking in sudden anger at another man with his sharpened hand-axe. Homicidal aggression is therefore peculiarly natural for man, the argument concluded.

In fact the argument is false from beginning to end. Murder rates among many species of animals are very much higher than in man, even when our wars are taken into account. So far from being especially strongly inhibited against killing, as required by Lorenz's theory, male lions often kill one another in fighting over the rights to a group of females. Among twenty-three adults and sub-adult members of two prides of Serengeti lions, two males died in fights in a period of three and a half years' intermittent observation.

Male lions sometimes kill females, too, while many lions are seriously wounded by the teeth and claws of their fellows. And when one group of males has successfully displaced another group they frequently destroy the litters of young cubs sired by their predecessors. About one in six of all lion cubs are killed by lions. Nor are lions exceptional. The growing list of murderous species now includes macaque and langur monkeys, hyenas, hippopotamuses and black-headed gulls, while infanticide also occurs among gorillas and chimpanzees. By comparison, humans appear surprisingly peaceable.

How could Lorenz, a Nobel-prizewinning expert on animal behaviour, have the story completely the wrong way round? People had simply not watched animals in the wild for long enough periods to detect the murders. 'I have been impressed,' E. O. Wilson of Harvard wrote in 1975, 'by how often such behaviour becomes apparent only when the observation time devoted to a species passes the thousand-hour mark. But only one murder per thousand hours per observer is still a great deal of violence by human standards.'

The British police records homicides at an annual rate of roughly ten per million of the population. If you were an observer monitoring a typical group of fifty humans you would have to wait on average a thousand years, not a thousand hours, before you saw the more-or-less deliberate killing of one human by another. In some countries, it is true, murder rates are much higher and many murders may in any case go undetected, notably infanticides. And if killings in wars, world-wide, amount to a lamentable two million a year on average, the annual rate at which humans take human lives may go up as high as six hundred per

million. In that case the mean observing time between one killing and the next in a group of fifty humans would be about thirty years. Compare even that with six weeks, which is what a thousand hours represents in aggregate.

If human beings are acquitted of being more murderous of their own kind than other animals, that must alter our perspective on human evolution. To make too much of the evidence that many of the early hominids met death by violence is rash, given at least two different species of hominids co-existing in East Africa two million years ago. Mayhem between two distinct species is a very different matter from killing your own kind. Yet the more colourfully Robert Ardrey and others portray our human ancestors as being enamoured of violence and perverting their skills in hunting food into the hunting of one another, the more powerful are the evolutionary antidotes needed to bring us to our present abhorrence of homicide.

Of the two available theories (Hamilton's family-orientated one and Trivers's give-and-take between non-relatives), the latter seems more necessary and less counter-productive in its side-effects. Give-and-take depends on remembered actions among intelligent beings who stay together for long periods. If Trivers is right, we should be filled with admiration and gratitude for our unschooled grandfathers and grandmothers who made it happen. It is a pity that the bones are silent on which of the hominid species that preceded us deserves most credit.

The 1970s have thus brought a rehabilitation of humanity, after the biological denigration that was so enthusiastically pursued in the 1960s. Apart from all the other skills and aptitudes evolution gave to us, our social behaviour is characterised by three great and interdependent evolutionary advances. The first is the demolition of barriers to sociability among vertebrates,

Cynthia...will you join
with me in the ruthless arithmetic
of gene survival?

by the spread of altruism. Secondly comes the reduction in the murder rate. The third advance is the almost total replacement of instinctive behaviour by learning from other human beings – the very essence of the human conspiracy.

Missing instincts

After they stood up and began using their newly-freed hands to wield sharp sticks and stones, the early hominids could afford to smarten up their mouths. Gradually they lost the big vampire-like canines of the apes. But that meant they were permanently committed to using such tools. The old aphorism about man being a tool-making animal needs elaboration. Tools are a man-making culture. The cosmetic dentistry was just an early stage in an accelerating process which entailed one of the most revolutionary developments in the history of life on Earth: the shedding of instinct and the invention of culture as a basis for living.

Hints of culture are perceptible in the more intelligent primates. Among the macaques of Japan a young female, a veritable Archimedes, discovered how to separate grain from grit by floating it on water, and taught her troop-mates how to do it. Chimpanzee infants learn from the adults how to prepare a stick and use it to fish termites from their nests. But rob those primates of such skills and their lives would be scarcely affected; they are luxuries. Strip a human being of his tools, his language and his picture of how the world works, and you would have a thoroughly ineffectual animal. This dependence means that the human conspiracy, whereby people join together and make people, is more than just a conventional political game; our survival as individuals and as a species depends upon it.

A human being inherits the ability to laugh, but there is nothing whatever for him to laugh at until he has learned from others what is normal and what is ridiculous. He is equipped with enormously talented hands, but he has no more to do with them than a monkey has until someone gives him a paintbrush or a screwdriver. All that is characteristically human. Other animals are well primed with 'instinctive' behaviour, although the greater their capacity for learning the more important is the part that learning plays in their lives. In humans, the learning part has become not only very important but indispensable. A baby is not the 'clean slate' of recent theory – he has too many special propensities and requirements – but he is a little like a questionnaire that has to be filled out, item by item.

The experiences of individuals cannot directly influence the genes they transmit to their children; experience affects heredity circuitously and slowly, by the better survival-value of certain versions of certain genes. For example, if seals started eating human children, thousands of years might have to pass before any 'instinctive' fear of seals could establish itself in the genes. By culture the adaptation to anthropophagous seals would be instantaneous, as the word spread and mothers showed their infants pictures of the dreaded carnivores. And by keeping infants safe from seals, the culture would actually negate any evolutionary pressure towards an instinctive fear of seals. This process resembles Jean-Baptiste Lamarck's discredited theory that accounted for biological evolution by the inheritance of acquired characters, and it is purposeful and swift in a way that Darwinian evolution never was.

The relationship between the local culture and the human brain is almost like that of male and female. This is not a frivolous simile. Long ago in the history of life on Earth organisms stumbled upon the reproductive device of dividing their genetic material into female and male packages, which had then to be brought together to make new individuals; this trick accelerated evolution hugely, by shuffling the genes and creating new selective tests of vigour. In human evolution, the genetic package was again rendered incomplete, but now ready to plug into the local culture. The culture itself became the equivalent of a genetic package.

As Clifford Geertz puts it, speaking of how human beings adapted to taxing conditions in the ice ages: 'A large part of mankind's inheritance is transmitted outside the skin by the culture in which a child grows up. That was the extraordinary new principle that entered human evolution during the ice ages and perhaps, if recent discoveries are any guide, even before.'

Geertz is one of the most respected of American cultural anthropologists, and holds his own among the mathematical physicists at the Institute for Advanced Studies in Princeton. He emphasises the way the individual human mind is impelled to find meaning in the world and its events, and yet is unable to function independently of the cultural symbols transmitted from one generation to another. A newborn baby, Geertz observes, is capable of living a thousand kinds of life but ends up living only one. Along the road he craves guidance from the traditions and values and moral codes of the society into which he is born.

The central lesson from the anthropologists' studies of exotic cultures is that human communities, all more or less viable in their circumstances, span a vast spectrum of social behaviour and beliefs. In contrast with the peaceful Bushmen are the fierce, bullying, battlescarred Yanomamos. The Yanomamos live on the border of Venezuela and Brazil, and preach violence to their children and engage in absurd duels wherein each combatant takes his turn to stand still, while the opponent whacks him over the head with a three-metre club. Behaviour ranges from matriarchy to female slavery, from cannibalism to avowedly strict vegetarianism, from free love to celibacy, from religious fervour to high scepticism, from the most intimate collaboration of all ages and classes to the fragmented and alienated labour of modern industrial states. Although many anthropologists search for universals in human behaviour others, including Geertz, regard the 'lowest common denominator' as less instructive than the oddities and richness of particular customs.

So where does that leave our biological biases? Where they belong: not as instincts but as needs and predispositions to learn some things more readily than others. Reconciling the natural science of human biology with the social science of cultures in action is not easy, because of the persistent reluctance on both sides to see the other's point of view. But the more thorough the elimination of instinct the greater, not the less, was the biological need for built-in devices to ensure that societies would form and social learning would succeed. What some of those devices are will become clearer in later chapters.

Belief and knowledge

Biology, psychology and social science are themselves parts of our cultures. It is worth pausing for a moment, to reflect upon the status of scientific enquiries into human social behaviour, in relation to the evolution of that social behaviour. I am a human reporting to you, the human reader, on what other humans are saying about us humans. My selection is, I hope, tactful and sensible, but each of us looks in a mirror that is distorted by his personal, ideological and professional prejudices. At least the scientists aim for consistency in the interpretation of various phenomena and they submit themselves (or are forced by their colleagues to submit) to the arbitration of observable facts. And

science never claims to be finished; an idea is only as good as the latest failed attempts to prove it wrong.

As one of the main strands of our cultures, science in its modern form is the newest, although it continues a long and cumulative human tradition of trying to understand the natural world by close observation. Common sense, political ideology and art are among the other resources that cultures possess for clarifying what goes on in the world. They are theoretically compatible with the scientific approach, although they are not always compatible in practice. The contrast is sharper between science and religion: between organised doubt and organised truths.

According to Clifford Geertz, reason and analysis fail to resolve oppressive paradoxes of life and death and evil, and fail to touch some of the deepest springs of human action. A cancer specialist may know exactly what a loved one is dying of, but his knowledge scarcely helps him to come to terms with bereavement. For reasons of this kind Geertz thinks the religious perspective will persist as long as men crave meaning. However bizarre they may seem to an outsider, the myths of a culture have deep meaning for its people.

The sacred symbols of religion, whether a cross or a feathered serpent, are dramatised by rituals and myths that relate the way the world is to the way people ought to behave. For Geertz, a religion is a system of sacred symbols which induce worshipful 'moods' (of exultation, say, or melancholy) and pious 'motivations', which may be, for example, courage, circumspection or tranquillity. A human being is a meaning-seeking animal and, from the chaotic events that create personal feelings of bafflement, pain or injustice, religion provides a human refuge, by denying that these feelings are characteristic of the world as a whole. Religious ritual, by concrete acts that bring religious conviction to the human plane, creates an aura of 'factuality' and

The kiss of Judas. In all religions, dramatic narratives strike emotional chords that common sense or science can scarcely begin to match. (Painting by Barna da Siena).

leaves the participants thinking that their moods and motivations are uniquely realistic.

Geertz strives to see religious beliefs in 'a clear and neutral light', leaving aside the question of whether their assertions are true. For some scientists, that is not good enough: however objectively the notebook of a cultural anthropologist records it, a belief that the world is flat is not interchangeable for a belief that the world is round. Sherwood Washburn of the University of California, Berkeley, is both a noted investigator of human evolution and a stern critic of 'prescientific' thinking.

Our hunter-gatherer ancestors had to act decisively, Washburn reasons. Accordingly, their brains evolved to be able to reinforce their judgements, imperfect though they were, with a necessary feeling that they were correct in some absolute sense. For example, prescientific treatments for disease are usually directed at driving out a supposed foreign spirit or substance, and the brain invests such customs with the feeling that they are useful and important. In the prescientific world nature was personified, and the misconceptions of gods, spirits, and magic were built into the fabric of every culture. The human brain reinforced these misconceptions with powerful emotions, demanding that they must be right even in the worst and most destructive of human actions. Thus beliefs, in Washburn's view, divide mankind and provide excuses for hatred and war. He thinks the time will come when primitive misconceptions no longer dominate human behaviour – he hopes it will be soon – because the customs which continue in the era of the H-bomb could not even control the bow and arrow.

These contrasting and forceful opinions about beliefs present a crucial question concerning the future of mankind that a science of human behaviour ought to help to resolve. If Washburn is right, an escape by human beings from their prehistoric preconceptions may, among other things, increase the chances that scientific understanding of human behaviour will take practical effect in helping us to behave better. But then Geertz and others will ask whether the price of reason is too high for human beings, who may find themselves leading uninspired lives in a clinical, bureaucratic world. If Geertz is right and humans cannot live satisfactorily without beliefs that they hold with deep conviction, then Washburn's fear remains, that beliefs will go on aiding hatred and war between rival groups. The substance and tone of competing religious and quasi-religious doctrines may need then more careful and critical scrutiny, not less.

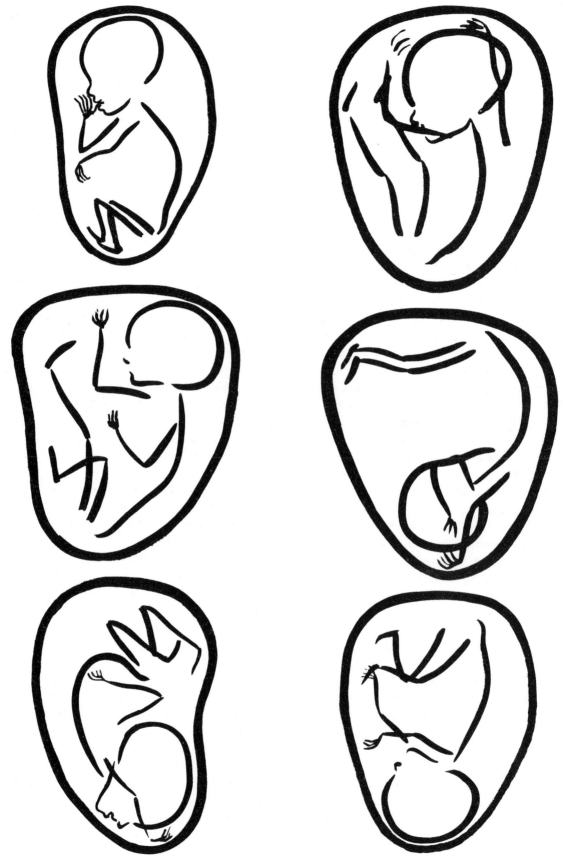

Habits before birth. Tracings from X-ray photographs show an unborn baby sucking his thumb and others contorting themselves in their efforts to find a comfortable position. A restless mother can accustom the baby to wakefulness at night.

2: Young Enlisters

When a baby begins life with the union of the mother's minute egg and the father's even smaller sperm, evolution and heredity have their last chance to register the genetic qualities appropriate for a new human being. The complement of genes needed by a human being is complete at the moment of conception. From then on the genes are on trial in their environment. Most remarkable, and least understood, are the master genes that govern the growth of the fertilised egg into a complex assembly of billions of living cells, each performing the task appropriate to its position in the body.

Sometimes the package of genes is defective in some conspicuous respect but the environment, too, can begin to have harmful effects. The baby has strong defences, but some infections suffered by the mother, notably rubella (German measles), can have serious consequences at critical periods of the baby's growth, while the effects of certain drugs like the notorious Thalidomide are too well known to need description. To what extent, or by what mechanisms, a pregnant woman's experiences of physical or mental distress may affect the growing foetus is still largely unclear, but the baby's heart rate can change abruptly when the mother's mood changes.

Behaviour before birth

The rhythms that most readily set people's feet tapping anywhere in the world resemble the human heartbeat. A recording of 'womb music', of the sounds that a baby hears before birth, has recently enjoyed some popularity as a way of inducing tranquillity in babies after birth. We all listened to the throb of our mother's heart and the rush of blood in her arteries, for months before birth. The episode of birth, important though it is, marks no abrupt change in the baby from a senseless creature into a human being. Detectable behaviour begins long before birth. The following brief account of it draws upon recent research by Sir William Liley and his colleagues in Auckland, New Zealand.

Thumb-sucking, for instance, can start almost as soon as the thumb is formed, six or seven months before birth, which may be why the habit is difficult to cure. Riding in his watery capsule the older unborn baby, when his ears begin to function, hears other noises besides the throb of his mother's heart. Muffled voices reach him from an unknown planet; doors slam and the baby is startled. The wind in his mother's gut sounds, at close range, like an artillery duel. The unborn baby is sensitive to disturbances. When doctors push a needle through the mother's skin into the uterus, to sample the fluid, the mother may be brave but the baby jumps in apparent pain. If, for medical reasons, chemicals that taste unpleasant are put into the amniotic fluid in which the baby floats, he will promptly stop sipping it. A Mexican doctor once introduced some air into the uterus to take a special X-ray photograph and the baby started crying.

The unborn baby sleeps and wakes, and he spends much of his time in a state which, in adults, corresponds to dreaming. If the mother is restless the baby will be restless too, trying to keep comfortable. The baby becomes aware of the alternation of night and day, but night-time with a restless mother can be busier for the baby than the daytime hours when she remains more or less upright. The baby puts much threshing of limbs and agile wriggling into seeking a comfortable position. All being well, the baby will find the head-down position most congenial and so be ready to emerge into the world in the approved fashion.

At birth, the baby participates actively, struggling while the mother labours. Human beings have a difficult birth because evolution has matched the size of the newborn human brain very closely to the limits of

'The normal mother of the normal baby primed at the moment of birth to fall in love with the newcomer.'

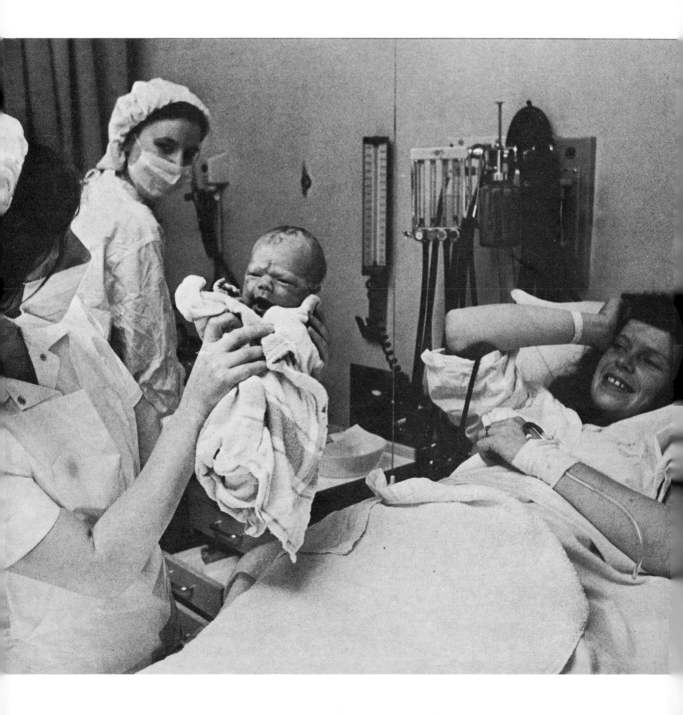

the mother's body. It is an alarming compromise: the mother's pelvis needs to be strong enough for walking and running and therefore not too capacious at the birth canal; but from the baby's point of view too small and immature a brain cannot be fully viable at birth. The mother is not alone in suffering pain at birth. Obstetricians are now inclined to regard the familiar cry of a newborn baby not as joyful exercise of the lungs, nor as a protest at his rude displacement from comfortable quarters, but as a response to a severe headache caused by having his skull squeezed through an aperture rather too small for it. To dismiss childbirth as something too 'natural' to fuss about does not take enough account of what a narrow squeak human parturition really is, or of how many mothers and babies die when skilled midwifery is lacking.

On the other hand, well-intentioned efforts to mitigate the pain with anaesthetics and analgesics may have had unlooked-for consequences. Both mother and baby are left drugged in the hours after birth. If the baby is dopey his initial responses to the world around him may be muted, including his responses to his mother. Even if she is clear-headed herself, a drugged baby may be a disappointing product at a moment when a mother is primed by her hormones and her exertions for an intense experience.

The importance of early contact between mother and baby is shown up most strikingly when it is lacking, as among premature babies who may spend a month or more under intensive care without any physical contact with the mother. When the baby is restored to her, the mother is likely to lack self-confidence, especially if the baby is her first. In the ensuing months the typical 'deprived' mother smiles less and holds the baby less than mothers who have had normal births. If she is divorced from her husband, she may willingly surrender the infant to him, a very rare occurrence in normal circumstances. After a year or more, many of the differences in behaviour between 'deprived' and normal mothers have disappeared, except that the 'deprived' mother continues to touch the baby less. But the separation of mothers and newborn infants may account for the statistics that show a premature baby to be in greater danger of battering by his parents than other children are.

A picture is emerging from research, of the normal mother of the normal baby, primed at the moment of birth to fall in love with the newcomer. That is an important event for both of them. And the baby, with his intricately wired brain and the biases built into him by evolution, is predisposed to be sociable and to learn what human social behaviour is all about, in the first instance from his mother. He is a ready-made conspirator and, from birth onwards, learning about the world and learning about people go hand in hand.

There's a clever baby!

In Western society the tricks of which a wholly untutored infant is capable went largely unnoticed before recent research took a fresh look. Every mother knew that the young infant was competent in nothing except crying and feeding and, to prove it, she wrapped the baby up snugly and laid him flat on his back. Yet some of the following performances have been observed within seconds or hours of birth, others during the first few weeks of life when the psychologists judge the babies to be still 'newborn' and free from any learning in the matters under investigation.

On hearing a sound a newborn baby can turn his eyes at once in the correct direction, to look for the source. That implies a brain already prepared (1) to deduce the direction of a sound from clues such as a slight difference in the time of arrival at the two ears,

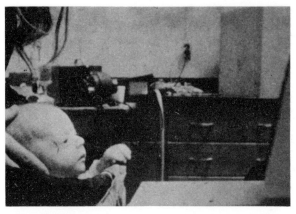

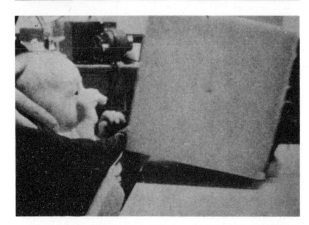

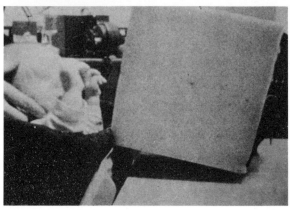

(2) to expect a visible object of some kind to be emitting the sound, and (3) to coordinate information from the ears with instructions to the eyes, so that a glance can be launched in the right direction. This occurs in a baby whose only previous use for his eyes was to observe a ruddy glow through the walls of his mother's body whenever she undressed in a bright room.

If his eyes locate an object the newborn will reach out for it, somewhat clumsily but in the right direction. When an object moves, the baby can track it with his eyes. If the object approaches close to him the baby will push back his head and raise his arms to protect himself; he does this when the object is about 30 centimetres away, regardless of the size of the object, so he is capable of distinguishing between a small object nearby and a large object far away, even though they form images of the same size in his eyes.

But some objects and sights are of greater interest to him than others. He spends longer looking at a striped pattern he has not seen before than at a plain surface or a pattern he knows well. He is especially interested in human faces, or objects and pictures that look like human faces. The baby seems to have a prior knowledge of what human beings look like. Also there is a sense in which the baby knows that he is a human being like the others he can see around him, otherwise there is no explaining the fact, mentioned at the opening of this book, that a baby a few days old will stick out his tongue when an adult sticks out his. A baby of this age can imitate various movements of face and hand, which implies that he possesses a built-in knowledge of where the various parts of his own body are, and how to control them.

By the age of two weeks a baby girl can distinguish between her mother's face and another woman's face (girls are running ahead of boys in many respects at this age). The behaviour that shows it seems to depend on the circumstances: in some test situations the baby spends longer looking at the mother; in others, she spends longer looking at the strange female face, and often turns her head aside from her mother, as if reproaching the mother for leaving her in a peculiar set-up where faces come and go. Either way, the baby's behaviour towards the two faces is different, showing that the baby has learned to recognise her mother by sight.

In fact, inside the floppy head of the newborn, who seems so helpless and often inattentive, a great deal of learning is going on, as the baby tries to make sense of the planet on which he has arrived. Some psychologists go so far as to say that our brains work harder and learn faster in the first few weeks than at any other period of our lives. Various experiments with newborns demonstrate their human capacity for learning.

Imagine that you are lying in bed and you hear a bell ring; then you hear a buzzer; then bells and buzzers at random. What you have to discover is that by turning your head left when you hear the bell, and right when you hear the buzzer, you will be rewarded with a penny. You have just worked that out and then the rule suddenly reverses – turn right at the bell and left at the buzzer. Three-day-old babies, rewarded with sips of sugar water rather than pennies, can solve the first problem in less than an hour and the reversal problem almost instantly.

A leading researcher on infant competence, Tom Bower of Edinburgh University, has summed up the recent findings as follows: 'Born with a high native endowment, the human infant has the potential to acquire new knowledge, skills and competence from the very moment of birth.' Thus the newborn baby displays the special human qualities described from the standpoint of evolution, towards the end of the last chapter. He is an incomplete animal, possessing various inborn skills and biological biases but relying on a powerful brain to find out what to do with them.

The viewpoints of evolution and infant psychology merge very well indeed. The human hallmark is adaptability. J. B. S. Haldane once speculated that the time might come when babies would be born speaking perfect English, but that would really be a big step backwards in evolutionary terms. For good practical reasons English, or any other language, changes from generation to generation far more rapidly than any genetic programme could evolve to keep up with it. If our language were in our genes we should each have an Académie Française in the head stubbornly resisting modernisation of the mother tongue. And just as there is a good reason why a baby should not speak at birth, so it is appropriate that he should not know spontaneously how to use a bow and arrow or hobble a mammoth. Otherwise he would be cluttered with obsolete skills just as he is, for instance, burdened with obsolete tastes for sugar and meat.

The immaturity of the newborn provides the very basis on which human cultures have been able to change so rapidly, whether amid ice ages or industrial revolutions. Each infant can be new-fashioned according to the prevailing technologies and mores of his society. In a rapidly changing world like ours his skills and interests can in due course become noticeably more 'advanced' than those of his parents. But with so much left unsaid by the genes, learning might be far too slow and difficult if the human head at birth were as empty as the behaviourists used to assert.

The inborn general competences concerning sights and sounds and body management are appropriate to the survival of the baby in all our cultures. But as the baby matures he has to relearn many of these competences, or at least reorganise them at a higher level of thought. More important than the tricks in which a

newborn baby shines are the biological biases in favour of attending to what other humans do, and being sociable towards them and eager to learn from them. The most peculiarly human method of social interaction is speech.

An interest in speech

How do you find out what is going on in a baby's mind? Even with adults, of course, you can never be sure of what someone is really thinking, but at least by interrogating him you can form an impression of his interests, opinions and emotions. The fact that babies cannot speak doubtless helped to foster outmoded ideas, either that the baby was empty-headed or that he was ravaged by intense emotions centering on his mother's nipple. Present-day infant psychology has a simple but ingenious way of arranging for the baby to report. It requires him to work a little, by sucking at an artificial teat which yields no food but controls sights or sounds. For example, the arrangement may be that a picture comes into focus in front of the baby if he sucks hard enough. The very fact that he is willing to do so shows that curiosity is at work and that small infants do not live by milk alone.

Whatever the intellectual reward for his efforts may be the baby will soon become bored with it and the sucking rate will flag – until the reward changes to something else. Then the baby revives and is soon sucking vigorously again. The interplay of curiosity and boredom provides the investigators with a powerful means of discovering what a baby can perceive as being 'something else'. If he does not notice a small change in a sight or sound presented to him he will go on sucking in a bored way; if his sucking accelerates it is a sure sign that he has spotted the difference. Perhaps the most striking discovery made with this

technique is that, on top of the other skills built into the infant's brain, one finds spontaneous recognition of the component sounds of human speech.

Tests on infants only a month old show that they can tell the difference between, for example, 'pah' and 'bah', and make just the same distinction as adults do. Picture the baby sucking the teat, which is wired for measuring suction. If he keeps sucking vigorously he will hear a sound of human speech – a 'pah' let us say, but not a very good 'pah', almost a 'bah'. Actually it is a sound synthesised by computer, so that its distinctive qualities are under the experimenter's control. When the baby realises that his sucking leads to the sound being repeated he sucks more energetically, at first. But after a few minutes of the same sound he begins to grow bored; his sucking rate falls to half or less.

Suppose now the experimenter changes the sound slightly, to make it what should theoretically be a clearer 'pah'. The baby does not hear any difference. Neither does an adult – a 'pah' is a 'pah', and the brain, charged with classifying speech sounds unambiguously, perceives distortions in them less readily than distortions in non-speech sounds. At any rate the baby is still bored. But alter the composition of the sound in a way that takes it across the boundary between 'pah' and 'bah', and the baby soon perks up, even though the physical change in the computer-generated sound is no greater than in the previous test. The baby starts sucking vigorously again to hear the new speech sound.

According to Peter Eimas of Brown University, who carried out these experiments, the human brain is equipped with an array of detectors pre-set by nature to register sounds of human speech. The analogy is with the system in the brain that begins the analysis of what the eyes are seeing. There, as justly celebrated modern researches have revealed, each brain cell responds exclusively to a line of a particular slope and length in the outside scene, as registered by the eye. A speech sound heard by the ear, so Eimas reasons, similarly provokes specialised cells in the brain.

Each baby seems to be born with such cells already wired and tuned to pick out the distinctive features of sound that, in different combinations, form all the speech sounds of every language on Earth. As it happens, other animals may make similar distinctions in speech sounds. Chinchillas, the South American rodents, can tell 'tah' and 'dah' apart, much as human adults do. Although the chinchilla may use a different brain mechanism, human language is possibly adapted to sounds that the brain can readily distinguish, rather than the other way about. Be that as it may, the young human is born equipped for language while the local culture has to supply the details.

This description – part discovery, part theory – also fits with the well-known ability of children to learn to speak a second language perfectly, while adult learners never seem to lose traces of their foreign accents. The Japanese adult who persists in saying 'I'm all light' instead of 'right' literally cannot hear the difference between 'l' and 'r' because 'l' does not figure in his own language. Eimas thinks that Japanese infants can tell the difference without difficulty. Instead of increasing with experience as a person grows older, skill with speech sounds actually diminishes. The child's ability to learn a second language with almost the same facility as his mother tongue has virtually switched off at puberty. None of that makes any sense at all if humans are seen as pure learners; but it is readily understandable as a biological process in which pre-adapted brain cells are either stimulated or allowed to atrophy through disuse, according to the speech sounds in which his culture bathes the child.

Language is so vital for human social life that evo-

lution has made certain, by speech-sound detectors and other means, that every child who has no gross defect shall learn to speak efficiently. Even an abandoned child growing up half-wild in the slums will become highly skilled in the prevailing language. This satisfactory state of affairs has been grievously obscured by pedagogues who judge people's linguistic performance by the standards of 'correct' language exhibited in formal classroom situations. Eminent Americans have been known to declare that some deprived black children do not know their own names, or the words for knife and fork, without pausing to consider that a child interrogated on these points may have many kinds of reasons for withholding the information.

Nearer the mark is the contrary assertion of an all-important biological and social conclusion: no human community, however deprived or unlettered it may be, lacks a rich, vigorous and subtle language. What it possesses may seem offensively corrupt to people who imagine that language begins and ends in grammar-books, lexicons and elocution classes. But if the tongue is seen instead as a limb for the management of other people's behaviour the only test that matters is whether a request, a complaint, a joke or an eloquent expression of emotion strikes home in a neighbour.

This digression into older life is not an aberration, because the study of how young children acquire their language has also been deformed by the pedantic view. The most exciting and productive trend in the study of the development of language rejects any notion that babies are slow students experimenting ineffectively with words until at last the day comes when they graduate by uttering a grammatical sentence. Instead, the baby is seen to be discovering, from the moment of birth onwards, how to communicate ever more effectively with other people, and an utterance that sounds meaningless on a tape-recorder becomes much more significant when recorded on a film that makes the social context clear.

The process begins with crying. Some psychologists suggest that the caretaker who ignores a baby's cry for no good reason may undermine from the very outset the baby's confidence in his ability to communicate his needs to other humans. Big differences in 'discipline' or 'compliance' are, though, found in mothers of different nations or generations. But note, in this connection, the match between a baby's cry and the adult brain, which is easily perturbed by the cry and, therefore, motivated to stop it.

The brain of the baby whose only utterance is a cry is far from deaf to articulate speech. A recent discovery comes from analysing films of babies frame by frame. On the first day of life an infant responds to human speech by making little movements of his body that correspond precisely to the segments and rhythms of the words. Now that is what adults do, too, when they are engaged in conversation, whether they are speaking or listening. Everyone notices the pronounced gestures, such as finger-wagging or arm-sweeping that often accompany speech but most of the movements are small and we are not aware of them. Similar patterns of movement are perceptible in any conversation in any culture and some of them are the same in newborn babies.

A newborn baby hearing an adult speak a sentence that starts 'Come over . . .' has been seen to act as follows. During the 'k' sound of 'come', which lasted for less than a tenth of a second, the baby swung his right hip outwards, stretched his left hip and moved his left big toe; there were also movements of the head, shoulders and arms but the catalogue becomes tedious. The important point is that several of the movements stopped or changed for the 'um' sound of 'come': for instance the left hip turned inwards and the big toe

stopped moving. On the 'oh' of 'over', the pattern of movements changed again, and now included a slow flexing of the right hip and right elbow – movements that reversed as soon as the sound changed to 'v'.

That is only a small sample of the bodily business going on while this infant listened to the words 'come over', but enough perhaps to give a sense of how remarkably it is synchronised with the speech. William Condon and Louis Sander of Boston University, reporting these findings in 1974, summed up their implications thus: 'If the infant, from the beginning, moves in precise, shared rhythm with the organisation of the speech structure of his culture, then he participates developmentally through complex, sociobiological entrainment processes in millions of repetitions of linguistic forms long before he later uses them in speaking and communicating.'

Conversation at two months

If a researcher asks a mother to talk to a two-month-old infant, she does not retort that it is a waste of time because the baby cannot understand her and will not be able to talk back at her for at least a year. She shows no surprise at the request and knows at once what is intended. She commonly puts her face about 30 centimetres from the baby's, the distance at which the child most easily regards her. Sometimes she addresses the child in 'baby-talk', sometimes in something approximating to adult language, but in any case with a good deal of repetition of words and phrases and with repetitive movements of her body and the baby's – perhaps a patting of the baby's hands in rhythm with her words. The baby likes a certain amount of repetition but boredom may set in; at that point the baby looks away and the mother, seeing him do so, alters her words and actions. The mother will think she is recapturing

the baby's wandering attention. From the baby's point of view, one could just as well say that by turning his eyes away he successfully manipulates his mother into performing a different trick for his entertainment.

Repeated movements may have instructional value. If the mother moves the baby's hand to and fro before his eyes, that may aid him in learning better coordination of hand and eye. If she speaks, moves and touches the child simultaneously, and does that a few times, he may profit from the experience of coping with information from several senses at once, and of integrating it. The apparent frivolity of the little scene of mother talking to baby is deceptive: the baby's brain is milking from the situation many kinds of knowledge, as well as the experience of confronting another human.

Some of the signals from the mother to the child are almost too quick for a bystander to spot; so are the reactions of the baby. In addition to the minute movements that any listener makes, in rhythm with the words, the baby face-to-face with his mother makes broader signals to her. Again, slow-motion films capture what the eye misses. From the tempo of the interchange, and the rhythmical ways the baby moves his hands and eyes and his face muscles, it becomes clear that mother and child are engaging in a real interchange – a conversation.

When his mother pauses the baby may draw his breath and hold it for a moment, just as if he were about to speak, and a tell-tale bubble made by a gentle expulsion of breath seems to signify a wished-for word. And the baby may raise his hand in a gesture quite different from the movement he uses to reach for an object, but characteristic of conversation before speech. Sometimes the baby stretches out his index finger, which may even be a foretaste of the finger-wagging done during adult speech.

These are mere techniques; the most conspicuous

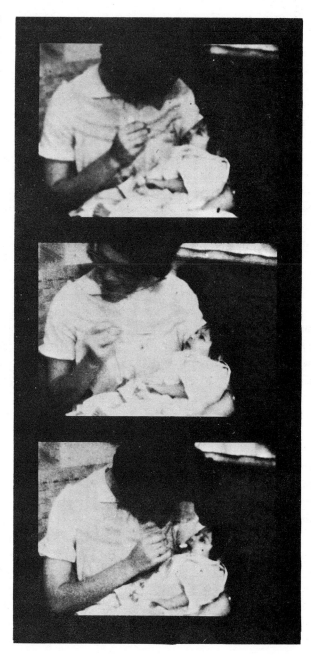

quality of the baby's participation in the conversation is its rhythm, expressed by hands, eyes and changes in facial expression, as if the mute baby already knows what talking is all about. The mother, too, is willing to respond to the baby's gestures. For example, if she drops her jaw in mock amazement every time the baby throws his arms back, she is letting herself be manipulated and giving the baby a chance to predict the consequences of his actions. The baby's evident satisfaction may come less from the attention and small kindnesses of his mother, than from understanding the rules of human interaction a little better and from learning how to influence, even if fleetingly, another human's behaviour.

I have followed the convention of referring to the baby as 'him', which allows a simpler distinction from 'her', the mother, but in this context reference to a female baby would be more appropriate, because girls are better at this pre-speech conversation than boys are. That may be the reason why parents are said to spend more time speaking to girl babies than they do to boy babies. Boys are more cavalier and more likely to interrupt the conversation on a whim, but the mother needs the gestured responses from the baby to keep her conversation going. So already, at this early age, social habits are beginning to feed on slight biological differences between the sexes, and amplify them. But among both girls and boys big differences in individual temperament show up in the quality and intensity of the pre-speech interaction.

Mothers and caretakers vary, too, in their performance. Some are not willing to interact with a child in the manner described, perhaps because they are too busy, or sick, or mentally disturbed. A general implication of the new ideas about what is going on inside the baby's head is that whether a mother is painstaking or offhand with her baby matters less than that she should be consistent. If the mother is unpredictable, or blows hot and cold, the baby may be discouraged about his ability to make sense of the world.

Psychologists and medical men can sometimes help in cases where the mother-child interaction is imperfect, using what they have learned by watching normal mothers in action. Unlike their predecessors who were officious and possibly injurious in their advice to parents in general, psychologists of the present generation concerned with mother-child interactions are thoroughly impressed by the skill that ordinary, untrained, unselfconscious mothers show in encouraging their infants to learn and be sociable.

Leading investigators on whose work this account of interactions is based put somewhat different theoretical interpretations on what they see. Hanuŝ Papouŝek of Munich regards the primary motivations of the young human as being directed towards solving problems, of which mother-management is only one. He speaks of a 'fundamental cognitive response system' at work in the child's brain; while Colwyn Trevarthen of Edinburgh postulates instead a primary sociability implanted by evolution. In his view the baby, endowed with an inborn capacity for interaction with humans, is striving consciously to establish social relations with his mother and other people.

On the interesting question of why babies smile there is a straight disagreement between Papouŝek and Trevarthen. Papouŝek thinks that the baby first smiles with self-satisfaction when he sees that his actions have an effect upon the world. If he smiles at his mother that is because she has responded to his actions. For Trevarthen, on the other hand, smiling is primarily a social signal and is used as such from the outset. As the human smile has evidently evolved from the silent bare-teethed face of monkeys and apes, among which it served first as a signal of submission and then as a

A special treat, three mothers at once. A mirror-system at Edinburgh University explores the mind of the infant, and finds the age at which he deduces that he only has one mother.

signal of friendliness, the latter view may seem more plausible. Other leading child psychologists think, though, that arguing about priorities, as between cognition and sociability, are futile at present and may always remain so. Both are strongly at work from the moment of birth.

Infant cosmology

A young baby experiences some difficulty in trying to understand the world he is in. People and objects come and go mysteriously, and many events occur that make no sense to him. At an early age he evidently thinks, for instance, that he has a generous supply of mothers. Although they all have the same face and appear to him one at a time, they do come in through different doors, wearing different clothes and smelling differently sometimes. Our notion of the baby's impressions is conjectural, of course, but his error is not. At Edinburgh University, Tom Bower's laboratory reveals this misconception in young babies, using mirrors.

The experimenters give the baby a special treat by showing him his mother and two mirror images of her, simultaneously. He is not particularly surprised about it and happily greets and interacts with each of his three mothers in turn. But after he is about five months old the same sight is surprising and disturbing to him. He knows by that time that a person is a single, variable object, and to have his reinterpretation confounded upsets him, in a way that a similar sight of the mother and two strangers does not.

Every human being at about five months of age deserves a Nobel Prize in physics. He has solved profound problems in natural philosophy, in discovering how the matter in the universe is organised into discrete, durable, movable objects. As babies approach this critical conclusion, tests with inanimate objects

Who is that? Not until about eighteen months does a baby realise that the coloured spot on the face in the mirror is actually on his own forehead.

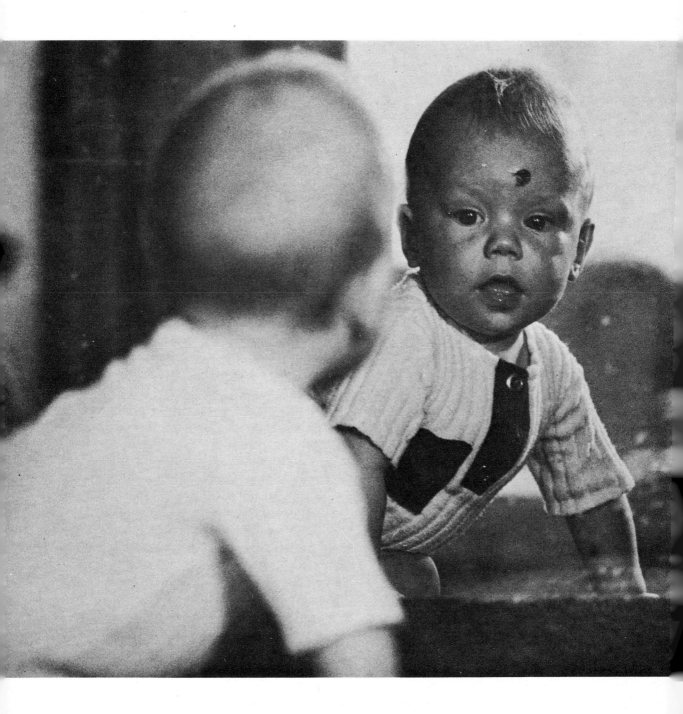

show fragments of understanding that have to be put together to reach it. The idea of an object occupying a place and the idea of an object in motion are at first separate and need to be merged. The assumption that identical objects seen in different places are different objects, is sometimes correct, but it has to be strongly qualified; they can be safely assumed to be different objects only if they are seen in different places at the same time.

The sight of the multiple mothers jeopardises precisely this hypothesis. Plainly, knowing that another person is a single entity is not just an intellectual advance but an essential step in grasping human relationships. So is the gradual clarifying of the child's awareness of 'self' revealed in part by other tests with mirrors. Put a spot of rouge on a child's forehead, and let him see himself in a mirror. Not until he is about eighteen months of age will he be sure that the rouge is on his own forehead.

An infant does not know the absolute truth about the world but has to work with his latest theory, like any scientist. Sometimes, in enlarging his knowledge and powers and reorganising them in a more general and controllable way, the child actually takes a step backwards in some of his powers. Bower emphasises that growing up is not a steady one-way progression from babyhood to adulthood. It is not necessarily always correct to suppose that the older the child is the smarter he must be.

A very young baby can reach towards a squeaking toy in the dark. At six months he ceases to do so. Indeed, parents of blind babies discover to their great distress that their children become less able to cope with the world at that age. By now the normal child, too, has lost the primitive, unified perception of the world with which he was born. He is having to learn afresh how to coordinate information from different senses and to

control his limbs accordingly, in a more deliberate fashion. And the Edinburgh group is finding that when older children learn to talk they actually sacrifice other mental powers.

When you hand a ball of modelling clay to a twelve-month-old child his arm drops, because he didn't know how heavy it was going to be. Take it back and hand it over again a couple of times, and the child learns to anticipate the weight of the ball. The arm stays steady. Then the experimenter rolls the same ball of modelling clay into a long sausage shape. Seeing it getting longer, the child thinks it must weigh more than it did before. When it is handed to him again, his arm flies upwards, because he has made too much allowance for the weight. That is as it should be, according to Jean Piaget, the prime authority on the development of mental powers in children. The 'conservation' law that a change of shape does not mean a change of weight is not supposed to be available to children until they are about seven years old. But the Edinburgh group goes on to contradict that long-cherished opinion.

The experimenters find that the error disappears at eighteen months only to appear again at about four and a half years of age. When the eighteen-month-old child sees the ball being rolled out into a sausage, he now knows quite well that its weight is not changing. And when the experimenter hands it to him, his arm correctly anticipates the weight. Other tests, changing the sausage into a ball, or using a folding ruler, give the same results. The problem is being posed, and knowledge tested, by actions rather than words. Tests in somewhat older children show that they have no difficulty with the conservation of weight – as long as they cannot fully understand the problem expressed in words. Using actions rather than words makes the test different from those in Piaget's studies. Nevertheless it is strange that children lose this grasp of the nature of matter, at about four and a half years of age. Now the child can take in, but not correctly solve, verbal questions about whether the sausage is heavier than the ball. In action tests his arm movements reveal the same error as the twelve-month-old baby made. He has now to reformulate his understanding of the world in a new system of thought – in language – and a couple of years will elapse before he can solve the problem formally, and make good the backwards step he took at four and a half.

During their long apprenticeship as human beings, children have to keep reorganising what they know into ever more complicated systems. As actions come within the system of language, performance may fall off sharply. When much older army recruits are told 'Swing your arms' this commonplace action in walking becomes quite difficult and individuals sometimes try to swing the arm and leg forward on the same side. Such setbacks might be a high price to pay for language, were it not so important for humans, as sociable, talking animals. Actions that can be explained to somebody else are often more valuable than cleverer actions that cannot be communicated.

A code to crack

Considered as a sample of prose, a small child's remark, 'Up!' is unimpressive and meaningless. But if you know that at that moment the child's mother is going upstairs, and that the effect of the remark is to make her return to the child and take him upstairs with her, then it is plainly a powerful communication, and one not available to animal species that have no signal for 'Up!' It is like a telegram, obscure in its parsimony to any prying eyes or ears but perfectly plain to the intended recipient. For the benefit of a third party a parent will often embellish a telegraphic utterance by a child,

giving a more articulate version of what the child was saying. There is no difference in principle from adult exchanges when, for example, the remark 'Idiot!' can be correctly reported as 'The other driver thought that the collision was my fault.' Such a down-to-earth view of language working in context has been regrettably unfashionable during the Chomskyan era in linguistics.

Historians may well say of Noam Chomsky that his great donation to human self-understanding was the sense of wonder that he broadcast about the creativeness of everyday speech. Virtually all human beings except the smallest continually utter sentences that were never uttered before, and they generally find them well understood. Looked at in the right way, the commonplace became thoroughly astonishing. During the past twenty years Chomsky, mainly at the Massachusetts Institute of Technology, has led a drive by linguists and psychologists to understand the processes of language. Dig deep enough, he said, beneath the surface forms and structures of any language and you will find the same universal grammar. Chomsky offered a package of explanations, the chief of which was the idea of a grammar machine inside our heads, essentially the same in all human beings. It allowed us, so the story went, to generate sentences and transform them at will – from a statement to a question, say – in accordance with grammatical rules.

Chomsky further supposed that humans alone possessed this faculty for generating true language. That is a minor issue except for the evolutionists and animal behaviourists. The various American experiments that have successfully persuaded chimpanzees to communicate with various kinds of symbols do not strike at the heart of Chomskydom. Yet by the mid-1970s, the psychologists who had marched off behind Chomsky were veering to another route and the linguistic theorists were in disarray.

A great deal of vigorous and sometimes hairsplitting controversy comes down to this: Chomsky's deep structure of language is too formal to have much discernible relevance to how people actually perform when they are speaking, or to why they bother to speak anyway. Grammarians of his school were astoundingly indifferent to the actual meaning and purpose of human utterances. So, the psychologists have now headed in search of meaning in language. They seem to be finding their way into human powers even deeper than language, as they redirect attention to the social context in which language functions.

A child has to crack the code of his native language and do it all in his young head, converting the gibberish he hears about him into a vocabulary and a set of complicated rules that he can himself use correctly. Children usually accomplish the task by the age of five. As grammarians cannot fully diagnose and write down the rules of effective language, the feat is formidable. Ten years later the same child may find formal teaching in French, say, very difficult to follow. Chomsky thinks the young child has a head start in the language business because the rules of grammar are innate to the human mind.

A quite different interpretation offers itself, more flattering to the young intellect. Jean Piaget and his colleagues in Geneva have for long argued that thought precedes language. Unfortunately the Piagetian approach offered no very clear way of relating the development of language to other symptoms of a mind in action. But, in the mid-1970s, Jerome Bruner at Oxford University has championed and clarified the same sort of view of language and its acquisition.

Besides being the most respected of American researchers into babyhood, Bruner also has an unusual awareness of research in other fields of psychology, and of comparative studies in animals. In proceeding to draw freely on his synthesis of ideas, I may be doing less than justice to other scientists, including Bruner's own students, but a service to the reader. Language research is a relatively new field for him, but Bruner's broadminded approach generates a picture of active young humans learning their language that is vivid and comprehensible. It further demonstrates the potential of a unified science of human behaviour.

Among the other primates Bruner sees the 'evolution of educability' – changes in social organisation from monkeys to apes to man which affect the way in which the young are inducted into the species. Experiments with baby monkeys separated from their mothers suggest that early social experience with other young monkeys is in a sense more important than mothering. Monkeys reared in isolation on the notorious wire mother-substitutes are very timid, but they are fully rehabilitated by a little play with normal peers – although of course the 'normals' would not be normal but for the mothering they experience.

Among chimpanzees the mother-infant link is more important and prolonged, lasting up to five years. From about eighteen months of age, the young chimpanzee is busy watching the behaviour of adults in all their activities and plainly learning from them. Chimpanzees resemble humans in another very significant respect. Unlike monkeys they can recognise themselves in a mirror and this implies, albeit indirectly, advanced selfconsciousness of the kind that allows a human to consider how his actions look to other people – perhaps the cornerstone of human social relations.

If the human infant has any head start in learning his language it comes, in Bruner's view, not from an innate grammar machine, but from the general rule-finding and code-cracking ability, visible in monkeys and apes yet exceptionally powerful in humans. Thought precedes talk. The child's thinking about the uses of words is greatly aided, though, by certain characteristics of his language. The code is, as it were, designed to be cracked.

Words in action

One of the plainest examples of how intellectual, social and linguistic performances are thoroughly interlocked comes in the child's confrontation with the words 'I' and 'me'. When the mother says 'I' she means herself; for the child to use 'I' correctly he must understand that from her point of view he is the other who will say 'I' when he speaks. Similar 'turning around' is involved in understanding and correctly using words like 'behind' in conversation – 'behind' from whose viewpoint? Imagine trying to write instructions on these points for a conversational robot and you may have some sense of the intellectual and social sensibility we take for granted in toddlers.

Language grows out of other and older aids to cooperative action among animals. If there are universals in grammar, Jerome Bruner argues, that is because any language must be well matched to psychological processes. Thus all languages direct the listener's attention to the topic before a comment is offered upon it, hence the basic subject-predicate form of sentences in all languages. Just as a person eyes an object, now forming an overall impression, now looking at details, so language permits rapid to-and-fro shifts in attention between the whole and the part.

Moreover, the categories of grammars are concerned with which agents carry out what actions on which objects with what effect. So language is primarily about attention and about action. Special features of human attention and action predispose the infant to success in cracking the code of language. They also predispose the mother and other people to help the infant most effectively, in his task, through playful episodes of joint attention and joint action.

Behind this interpretation lurk several important suppositions about what the child can do even before he is old enough to speak. He can distinguish people from things and himself from other people. He has intentions and he understands that other people have intentions that may or may not coincide with his own. These are not assertions to be made lightly, but childish persistence, for example, is a fairly clear sign of intention, while refusal to cooperate with the mother may imply recognition of a conflict of intentions.

The mother's different 'tones of voice' for commands, questions and statements set up different expectations in the child, and when he comes to speak he uses the same prosody. Above all the child is quick to distinguish experiences shared with other people from other kinds of experience, to know for example whether a particular action by his mother is supposed to involve the child or not. Here, surely, is the onset of the human ability to put oneself in another's shoes.

A mother interacting with her baby will tend to look at whatever the child seems to be looking at; conversely an infant four months old is able to look at what the mother is looking at. Later, the remark 'Oh look!' from the mother will evoke this gaze-following response more readily. Once both mother and child are looking at the same thing, mutual attention exists, and a comment or action from the mother follows naturally.

The child first uses words to achieve or to comment upon actions undertaken jointly with his mother or another person. He starts with words that are clearly agents, actions or objects: 'Mommy' as an agent who is supposed to do something; 'gone' as the most striking action performable by agents; and 'spoon', 'milk' or 'Mommy' as the objects to which something is happening. What the 'something' is is usually clear from the context. When the child can first put two words together, they are combinations of agent and action ('Mommy push'), of action and object ('bite finger'), or of agent and object ('car garage'). The idea of possession emerges naturally from the realities of control ('aunt car').

Bruner and his Oxford colleagues observe children through the period of life in which they first begin to speak. The research involves videotaping their interactions with their mothers in the home setting, at regular intervals. Observations start from seven months of age, when a child has no conventional language. Already a great deal of signalling, rather formalised and recurrent, passes both ways between mother and child. All the mothers taking part in the research have proved to be well-accustomed to interpreting the child's signals.

Some mothers tend to respond by helping the child achieve what they seem to be intending to do; others, by helping him to find out more about an object that seems to interest him. Bruner is particularly struck by words such as 'There!' commonly uttered by mothers in a special tone of voice that marks the completion of an action; these markers are equivalent to the end of a spoken utterance and a signal that a new sequence of action can begin. Although mothers take the initiative at the beginning of play, they are skilful at encouraging the child to take a more active part.

In a typical sequence of events with Ann, a nine-month-old child, the mother holds out her hand for a block that the child is playing with. Ann puts the block in her mother's hand but does not let go. Several minutes later Ann takes hold of her mother's hand and puts the block into it. The mother says 'Thank you' but the child still does not let go. After more of this kind of thing, the mother takes the object forcibly. Ann then

reaches out with a cry and the mother hands the object back. At this age the child incorrectly says 'kew' when handing over an object; she is imitating her mother's marker 'Thank you'. Two months later, Ann is saying 'kew' when she is receiving an object, and 'look' when handing one over.

Care and privilege

'Put the *lid* . . . (*mother points and pauses*) . . . on top of the basket (*mother points to basket*).' This instruction to a sixteen-month-old boy is cited by Gordon Wells as an example of the care that people take to make sure that they are understood, of how speech is surrounded by shared activity and gestures, and of the sorts of communications that a young child experiences many times a day. Wells is another proponent of the social context, as crucial for understanding the nature and acquisition of language. At the University of Bristol he is elaborating a theory of how the child learns to encode in a language his understanding of experience. Wells is also carrying out a study of language development, starting with somewhat older children than Bruner's – fifteen months onwards.

Altogether 128 children are involved. Each child wears a harness with a radio microphone while a tape-recorder samples his speech for ninety seconds every twenty minutes during the course of a day, and the procedure is repeated every three months. No observer is present in the home during the day, but in the evening the mother hears the tape and explains the context of each sample. From time to time the children's powers of language are tested more formally. One finding so far is that the children do not start talking about their inner feelings and thoughts until they are nearly two and a half years old; before then all remarks concern the outside world. Another is that two-thirds of all verbal exchanges between mother and child turn out to be started by the child (at three and a half years).

Wells has practical as well as fundamental objectives in mind. He wants to find out why some pre-school children are more advanced in their speech than others. In Britain, the main hypothesis up for contest is that of Basil Bernstein of London University, who asserts that social underprivilege translates rather directly into linguistic underprivilege, which in turn helps to produce social underprivilege in the next generation. To affirm, as many linguists do, that the language of the working class is splendidly rich, does not dispose of the problem, if working-class children are being judged by middle-class teachers and employers. The central issue is whether or not working-class mothers and caretakers, because they are too busy perhaps, or not articulate in appropriate ways, omit to give the child certain kinds of linguistic experience. At the time of writing the main study at Bristol is only half completed. The pilot study, which involved eight children in varied social backgrounds, gave no evidence of any class effect in the rate of linguistic development.

The most striking difference that showed up was consistently faster development in first-born children, plainly related to more time spent by the mothers in talking and playing with them – a difference to which mothers with younger children regretfully admit. There was a sex difference too. The boys seemed to talk more in the context of 'mothering' (bathing, dressing, feeding and so on) while the girls were more voluble in the context of 'joint enterprises' with their mothers.

Class differences showed up a little in the kinds of conversations in which the children spoke the most. There was more emphasis on the giving and receiving of information, including deliberate teaching about language itself, in the middle-class homes – although

with no discernible effect on the children's rate of progress. The main study also shows that middle-class children talk more about books and reading, and class differences are becoming plainer.

Jerome Bruner has little patience with notions about 'enriched' and 'deprived' environments that envisage the child as the passive recipient of objects to look at and fiddle with. What matters is nurturing the child's attempts to achieve goals, with objects and with other people. Bruner suspects that 'cultures of failure' can result from prolonged poverty. A lack of leisure and material resources, perhaps coupled with a policy of preventing a child being over-ambitious, may lead adults to be forever saying 'Stop that' or 'No you can't' to children, until they give up trying. When encouragement and interaction are all-important, it matters not at all whether a child and mother play with an expensive fire engine or an old coffee can – except that you can do many more significant things with a coffee can.

After so many references to mothers and babies, a comment about mothering may be appropriate. Much of the past twenty-five years' research into mother-infant interactions was set rolling by John Bowlby's hypothesis that the separation of mother and infant was traumatic for the child. This notion, which had Freudian connotations, carried the political implication that a mother ought not to go out to work when her children are young. A quarter of a century later the bond between mother and child looks more robust than Bowlby implied and babies seem well able to adapt to other caretakers, at least after the first few weeks of life. But the research also makes abundantly clear the practical importance for the child's development of the 'tender loving care' that comes most reliably from the mother: paying ample attention to the infant, playing with him, talking to him. So the political issue is redirected from the desirability of mothers working to

Quality of caretaking. Although the natural mother may be in some ways biologically attuned to her baby, others can supply the love and attention that the infant needs for his mental and social development.

the quality of baby-minding in her absence. But even here one should not make hasty judgements about 'right' and 'wrong' treatments.

Among the Bushmen and many traditional agricultural communities in Africa, small babies are far more 'stimulated' than in, say, the United States; they are with their mothers all the time, in a sling, watching the world go by. But in other countries (the Netherlands for example) babies receive much less 'stimulation' than American babies do, including much less playful interaction with their mothers. It is notable that Americans, who go through more public agonising about their child-rearing practices than any other nation, fall securely in the middle of the range, in mental stimulation at least. These international comparisons suggest that all sorts of practices by mothers or child-minders can produce wholly satisfactory people. But they may well be different people: more or less tranquil, more or less sociable, more or less curious, in accordance with the norms of their societies.

Just for fun

The way in which a child organises other kinds of skilled actions suggests useful parallels and contrasts with the acquisition of language. A child reaching for an object does so at first in a clumsy, ineffective way. The abilities noted in newborns fall far short of reliable action. The very young child may have the ingredients of an action but be unable to deploy them with their correct sequence or timing. For instance, he may close his fist before his hand reaches an object. The baby's intention may be plain enough – perhaps he has his mouth open ready to put the object into it – but success eludes him. Eventually by a continual interaction of intentions, plans, monitored progress and monitored outcomes, the child becomes capable of grasping an

object, and of correctly adjusting his actions to its size and distance.

Once that is accomplished, and the child can grasp objects more or less at will, he can take the skill for granted – it becomes what Jerome Bruner calls a 'subroutine', by analogy with subsidiary units incorporated into a computer program. The child can then move on at once to finding out what can be done with an object in hand, for example moving it about, or showing it to someone. The more advanced skills can, in their turn, become subroutines fit for combining and modifying, whether in playing a game or in making something. But if you try to demonstrate a complicated process of assembly to a child who cannot manipulate the pieces – who does not possess the subroutines – you are wasting your time and his. Gradually the child constructs his skilled actions by the proper arrangement in serial order of a variety of subroutines.

And so it is with language, up to a point. There is the same progression to higher levels of skill, each of which can be taken for granted as the child moves on to the next stage. There is the same problem of timing – of fitting a remark into the right place in an activity, or of putting words in the correct order. But there is one very important difference. Precisely how a child picks up an object does not matter very much, but how he waves goodbye to strangers has to fall within the range of gestures that are generally interpreted as such a wave. How he speaks, and eventually composes sentences, also has to conform very strictly to the conventions of his society. The test of success is no longer the child's satisfaction with his own performance, but the ability of other people to recognise his communication – to understand him. That is what the child has to be able to monitor. And that is why early experience of pseudo-conversations before speech, and experience in observing the effects of gestures on a willing adult stooge,

I have correctly adjusted my actions to the size and distance of this problem.'

Goo

seems a very appropriate preparation for language acquisition.

These situations of mother and child are typically playful. Here we encounter another of Bruner's favourite themes, which extends well beyond matters of language. What play and language have in common is the existence of rules. There are internal rules about the correct order in which events are supposed to happen, and a sense of activity broken up into segments by the completion of a 'turn' in a game, or the end of a sentence in language. There are social rules, too, about turn-taking and role-playing. And play involving language brings special benefits for the infant.

A toy can undergo operations, to the accompaniment of remarks about who is doing what to it. The operations and words can be repeated at will, and then varied or reversed, bringing out the similarities between the manipulation of objects and the manipulation of sentences. The words are a conspicuous part of the game, which therefore directs the child's attention to the words themselves and what you can do with them. And because it is all 'just for fun', experiments and errors bring no fateful consequences.

The impetus for present studies of play in humans came from observations of the playfulness of monkeys and especially of apes in the wild. People who had dismissed childish activities as a human frivolity could hardly suppose that nature was frivolous, in allowing young animals – and adults too – to spend so much time and energy in play, to no apparent vital purpose. Domestic kittens could have prompted thoughts about the importance of play, centuries ago, but the hint was not taken.

Monkeys have a reputation for mischief but, in fact, their playfulness is limited, both in its scope and in its confinement to an early phase of infancy: adult monkeys do not fool about. In chimpanzees, play continues into adulthood and mothers play with their babies. At the age when infant chimpanzees are watching adults closely they will begin to reconstruct adult behaviour in their play. But the character of play in chimpanzees as well as humans is much more creative than mere imitation. For instance a chimpanzee youngster with nothing but a twig to play with may tear off its leaves, throw it, rub himself with it, poke it into holes and bend it until it breaks. He is finding out what you can do with a twig.

Children solve problems more efficiently during play than in the course of more formal instruction or testing. One experiment to this effect, done when Bruner was at Harvard, involved children aged three to five who had to clamp two sticks together to reach a prize. Uninstructed children allowed to play with the sticks solved the problem just as reliably as other children to whom the whole procedure had been demonstrated, and twice as often as children instructed more formally in the use of the clamps. Very similar benefits of playing with materials before the posing of a problem have shown up in tests with chimpanzees. Children in play also persevere longer and, because they are less tense, they probably think and learn better.

Baboons and chimpanzees make signals to indicate when they are playful. They open their mouths wide without showing their teeth – an evolutionary precursor of the human laugh – and move with a clownish gait. Then friendly chasing and wrestling can ensue. Harmless movements may be exaggerated, and harmful ones moderated. But if, unluckily, the other animal fails to register the signal, a real fight breaks out. Catherine Garvey of Johns Hopkins University describes the same contrast in children between three and five years old, standing beside a wooden car which they both want to ride. They can shove in earnest until one is displaced; or, to the accompaniment of giggles and smiles, they may stage a playful tournament, carefully taking turns to shove and be shoved, although not very hard.

The taking of turns is one of the indicators that play is in progress; the analogy with conversation has already been mentioned. The smiles and the moderation of harmful movements in play are as plain in the behaviour of apes as they are in children, and a bias providing for play must be counted a part of our biological nature. But small humans quickly achieve an imaginative richness in play to which no ape could aspire. They improvise rules and roles, and then try to keep to them. Here is an example from one of Garvey's tapes that shows the readiness of a four-year-old to accept correction about his role:

'First child: Pretend you're sick.
Second child: OK.
First child (*into phone*): Hey, Dr Wren, do you got any
    medicine?
Second child: Yes, I have some medicine.
First child: No, you aren't the doctor, remember?
Second child: OK.
First child (*into phone*); I need some medicine for the
    kids. Bye. (*turns to other*) He hasn't got any medicine.
Second child: No? Oh dear.'

Different kinds of language

For all the talk about 'universals of grammar' languages obviously differ greatly in their superficial constitution. In some, including English, the sense is conveyed primarily by the order of words: 'Julius accuses Maria' or 'Maria accuses Julius' have quite different meanings. In other languages a lot of the sense is built into the words by 'inflexions', so that their order becomes less

The age of make-believe. The play of young children involves real rules about imaginary situations.

important: 'Julius Mariam accusat' and 'Mariam Julius accusat' have exactly the same meaning in Latin and both are grammatically correct – the marking of Maria with the final 'm' being the key. Another leader of the 'new wave' in psycholinguistics, Dan Slobin of the University of California at Berkeley, has been conducting a cross-cultural study of four groups of children growing up and learning their different mother-tongues.

If it is correct to say that language follows thought, and if the strategies available to a child for thinking are universal, then universal ways of acquiring knowledge should show up in children learning to talk anywhere, despite the great differences in the languages. The languages compared in the study are English (a word-order language), Serbo-Croatian and Turkish (highly inflected languages) and Italian, which is intermediate. Field-work has been carried out in Dubrovnik, Rome and Istanbul, with children from two to four and a half years of age. A main conclusion is that one language is not easier to learn than another. In other words children are equally adept at mastering inflexional and word-order systems. That is not to deny notable differences in the pattern of events.

For instance the inflexions of Turkish are very regular and easy to hear: Turkish children master them by two years of age while their opposite numbers are still struggling with the more unruly inflexions of Serbo-Croatian or English at five. When the rules are difficult, children alter them to suit themselves. Typically they overgeneralise the rules – saying for instance 'he bringed' instead of 'he brought' by quite intelligent analogy with other verbs. In this fashion they manage to convey their meaning successfully though 'incorrectly' for a couple of years until they have it right. The Turkish children have difficulties of another sort. While it is very easy in the Indo-European languages to make relative clauses – to go from 'Harry bought the doll' to 'Give me the doll that Harry bought' – the means in Turkish are complex and Turkish children lag two or three years behind their foreign colleagues.

By five years old a child possesses the basic apparatus of his language, which will serve him into adulthood. If that is to occur universally, by and large languages must be equally difficult to learn. But each generation modifies the language in subtle ways. One notable change has been recorded among Pidgin speakers of Melanesia. Where adults for the future tense say 'I by-and-by go home', children are saying 'I b'go home': they are evolving an inflected future tense ('go'/'b'go'). Languages may go through cycles of lesser and greater inflectedness, as speakers and learners continually test their effectiveness and speed.

While a child's command of grammar remains weak, he needs the context of real action to make himself understood. But language does not remain for long bogged down in its contexts. Once the conventions of grammar are available to the child, language becomes a magic carpet that can instantly carry speaker and listener anywhere in space and time, to fairyland or into absurdities, whether jokes or lies. In its printed form, language becomes wholly separate from real interactions between people: you who are reading this book have no idea of how I am writing it, nor of how many amendments I have made to this paragraph.

Language has at last a secure and central place in the study of human behaviour. It is the primary means of discovering what other people are thinking and feeling. Words loom large in everyday thinking and help to give precision to vague thoughts while, as a symbolic system, language serves the human intellect in many of its highest achievements. In any case, a large part of human behaviour consists of talking to other people. As a web that holds groups and societies together, language modulates the social behaviour of individuals, sometimes with the force of magic, and often playfully.

We have considered, so far, aspects of behaviour that are widespread in our species, reflecting our common evolution and the normal course of infancy. But human individuals differ in fascinating ways, and those differences are a source both of richness and of iniquity in our societies. A question of fundamental importance to social behaviour, affecting all our hopes for improving human life, is just how malleable people are. To what extent do social circumstances and pressure fix what an individual shall be like, and how far do inherited characteristics of individuals assert themselves despite society. The next chapter reviews some of the latest findings about effects of heredity and effects of culture before we turn, in the succeeding chapter, to the relations between individual, inter-personal and group behaviour revealed by scrutiny of what humans actually do.

Race relations—South Africa. The laws of nations give substance to discrepant theories about human nature—in this case preventing blacks from even walking on the same public stairway as the whites.

3: Nature and Nurture

'What are you going to do with this knowledge when you have it?' That is the challenge thrown down by political radicals in American science who systematically oppose any research into hereditary influences on behaviour. In 1975 they succeeded in stopping research in the Boston area into the consequences of the XYY chromosomal error. This is the condition in which boys are born with an extra Y (male) chromosome over and above the normal complement of 46 chromosomes carrying the messages of heredity. There have been reports, warmly debated among the experts, that such males have a strong tendency to finish up as violent criminals. The radicals fear the consequences to a person of being labelled from birth as a potentially dangerous freak.

They go further: it is unethical to conceal from the parents results of a chromosomal test in a child; to tell them of a peculiarity is also unethical, because it is bound to affect their own behaviour towards the child. In this fix, the argument goes, the ethical scientist can only abandon the idea of such testing. The scientists doing the research in question retorted that they were aware of the ethical problems and that they had no wish to stigmatise anyone. The XYY boys may face special problems in childhood, including speech and reading difficulties. Parents respond sensibly to advice about such problems, but the advice must be founded on systematic investigation. Following an enquiry the faculty of the Harvard Medical School overwhelmingly endorsed the XYY project. Yet personal and potential legal pressures on the chief researcher became intolerable and shortly afterwards he stopped the project which had been running for seven years. I have discussed the issue with both sides and consider this outcome to be thoroughly regrettable. Even though the general fears of the radicals are not groundless, there is reason to think that open-minded research on behavioural genetics will have humane consequences.

Down with dogma

The geneticist's approach to human talents and behaviour has a long history of exploitation by the political far right, which has sought genetic differences between rich and poor and between different races in order to justify iniquity. Allegations about such differences fed the Nazi ideas about eugenics and helped to inspire the massacre of the European Jews. When the horrors of Auschwitz and the other extermination centres came to light, scientistic racism understandably went out of fashion for a couple of decades.

It reappeared in the United States in the late 1960s following the pronouncements by Arthur Jensen that the lower intelligence-quotient scores achieved by blacks as compared with whites were mainly due to hereditary differences between the two races, and not to differences in their social circumstances. Later, Hans Eysenck in Britain offered an explanation: the American Negroes were descended from Africans who were not smart enough to avoid the slave-traders. Gratuitously he went on to ascribe the well-known stupidity of the Irish to the fact that their forefathers were not smart enough to emigrate. William Shockley, the American physicist, suggested loudly that people with low IQ scores should be paid not to breed.

All that constituted a scandal of the first order. Now that the dust has settled (if indeed it has) one can safely say that the available data permit no conclusion whatever about hereditary differences in intelligence between blacks and whites, that the importance of genetic determinants in intelligence has in any case been exaggerated, and that there is a superabundance of environmental, medical and social factors, in the conditions in which American blacks are born and grow up, to account for their poorer performance in IQ tests. In any case, IQ testing itself has been greatly discredited.

Race relations—United States. Bussing, the legalised daily transport of children, attempts to mix the races at American schools and equalise their experiences, but it has become a focus of racial tensions and civil strife.

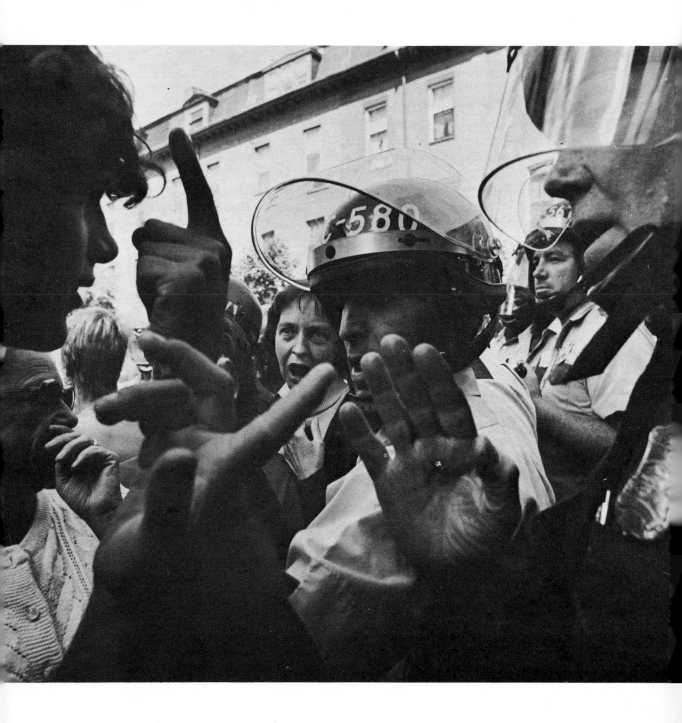

Identical twins – different fingerprints. Here is the simplest demonstration that genes are not all-powerful.

To dispose of the Jensenist contention has, though, required years of research and polemics by able scientists. They still fear that the damage has been done – that the public that got the Jensen message is not very receptive to technical counter-arguments that revolve around comparability and statistical significance. And many scientists are understandably touchy about any research which looks for genetic differences that may underlie differences in human behaviour.

The question, 'What are you going to do with this knowledge?' forces attention to the motives behind such research, both of the scientists themselves and the agencies that finance them. Underlying the politics are deeper issues. Why are human beings so anxious to measure one another's characteristics and to put labels on people? Part of the answer is that assessments of others are an unavoidable part of everyday human social behaviour; you could say we are all obsessed about differences. Associated with this obsession are questions of stigma and of human group allegiances – considered in the next chapter.

But why try to dig out genetic factors to help explain the differences between people when conspicuous environmental factors are crying out for attention? The modern answer ought to be that we cannot expect to understand any aspect of human behaviour properly unless we recognise that humans are products of their biology and their experience working together. That means setting aside dogma, and with it political predeliction or hypersensitivity, on both sides. What the Jensen affair demonstrated was a combination of technical and political ineptitude, and not the impropriety of behavioural genetics. The other side of the penny, though, is that heredity, of the species, a population or an individual, ought never to be regarded as a condemnation. Human beings, far more than other animals, routinely transcend their biological endowment.

More profoundly, the 'environment' in which individuals live consists largely of other people's behaviour and attitudes, which may themselves be partly influenced by heredity. Opinions about the malleability or incorrigibility of human beings affect the policies of individuals and societies towards a person, which in turn affect that person's circumstances and resulting behaviour. Our estimates of the possible direction and speed of social change depend on our assumptions about how people will respond, and any policy of reform which understates or overstates the causes and importance of individual differences in behaviour is liable to fail. For supposedly rational animals, ignorance, wilful or otherwise, cannot be a virtue. Better knowledge of genetic traits and environmental influences can help us deal more wisely with one another or be used to put particular groups at a disadvantage. That is always the way with knowledge, whether it concerns the forces of the atomic nucleus or the workings of the mind. Knowledge does not guarantee wisdom but is an indispensable part of the environment for wisdom.

The amount of genetic variation among humans turns out to be far greater than most biologists imagined even ten years ago. One of the key discoveries of the new molecular genetics is that there are alternative versions of almost every gene. Except for identical or 'monozygotic' twins, who come from the same fertilised egg, all human beings differ thoroughly from one another in their bodily make-up, because of the way the genes are shuffled and reshuffled from generation to generation. Each person represents a combination of genes never tried out before and even in identical twins the course of development is not identical so that, for example, their fingerprints are not the same. The vast differences between individuals in any one family, population or country greatly exceed the differences between populations in various parts of the world.

Just as everyone's face is subtly different, so is everyone's behaviour and accomplishments, and it would be surprising indeed if the genes had nothing to do with those differences. On the other hand there are general reasons for supposing that in those aspects of human behaviour that matter most, including intelligence, powers of language and sociability, strong evolutionary pressures will have been at work, keeping the potential quality high in all except plainly defective individuals, who tend not to breed anyway. And social factors obviously have enormous influences in determining whether a particular set of human genes turns into a stupid hero or a brilliant crook.

Scottish cattle, English meadow

The biological fact that all human beings are different has been used by some to ridicule the 'self-evident truth' stated in the American Declaration of Independence, that all men are created equal. But 'equality' and 'inequality' are human notions about human beings. Some people can run faster than others; one man may invent the quantum theory while another fails to learn to read; these are differences of the sort on which natural selection or human eugenicists might conceivably act. Any denial of the proposition that all men are created equal involves an arrogant assumption that one knows the most desirable human qualities, not only now but for all time.

It implies that human beings might agree upon precisely what qualities are more important than others. They would have to be very few in number, otherwise too many people rated high on one consideration would score low on others and confusion would reign. Perhaps one might take IQ scores and, in view of our overcrowding, smallness of stature. The ideal person is then a brilliant midget. But that just reflects prejudices

of the proposer, and ignores kindliness, humour, manual dexterity, resistance to disease, fertility and a thousand other qualities. In different cultures, or in different periods in the same culture, different qualities are esteemed. A major environmental change, such as the new ice age that may occur soon, could drastically alter the significance of different human qualities in the biology and sociology of survival. In any case, how are you going to apportion to any one individual the sheer value to the community of having individuals with diverse interests and talents? Perplexities of this kind help to safeguard the legal principle of equality, and also deny us any simple solution to another ancient issue.

The question of nature versus nurture, of the relative importance of heredity and environment, has generated contention and conflict for thousands of years. In our century, while the racists, Social Darwinists and eugenicists have voted for nature, communists and behaviourists have said that nurture is all and a perfect society will create perfect humans. Virtually all scientists have felt obliged to pay lip-service, at least, to the notion that both nature and nurture are at work, but many have then gone ahead in their genetic or environmental preoccupations as if there were no interplay. Other scientists who have tried to resolve the nature/nurture issue have resorted to different methods.

One idea is to assign numbers: for example, you say that sixty per cent of the variation in a particular characteristic is due to heredity and forty per cent to environmental differences. This is the approach used by Arthur Jensen and many others, but there is a big snag. The amount of variation due to the two causes depends on the environment; in consequence the results of such studies apply only to a particular population living in a limited range of environments. So attempts to resolve the nature/nurture issue by using statistics are likely to be meaningless, except as an easily misinterpretable description of a purely local situation.

In a little book *Heredity and Politics*, published in 1938 when anti-semitism in Germany rather than the confrontation of white and black was the great racial issue, the geneticist J. B. S. Haldane produced a simple argument. He showed that no general answer could be given to the question: 'What is the relative importance of nature and nurture?' He considered two races or groups, A and B, in two environments, X and Y. For ranking the races according to their achievement in some respect, he set out four main possibilities, as shown in the diagram. 'The enumeration is so simple that no one has ever troubled to make it,' Haldane wrote – to which we may add that few have troubled to make it since.

An example of the first possible kind of interaction of different heredities and environments is provided by

J. B. S. Haldane's demonstration of nearly forty years ago that there is no general solution to the nature/nurture problem. 1, 2, 3 and 4 refer to the rank order of some achievement, and the text explains the examples.

		X good diet	Y bad diet	
races and	A mastiffs	1	2	A surpasses B in both environments but
weights	B dachshunds	3	4	X is better for both

		X English meadow	Y Scottish moor	
races and	A Jersey cattle	1	4	A surpasses B in X
milk-yield	B Highland cattle	2	3	B surpasses A in Y but X is better for both

		X ordinary school	Y remedial school	
races and	A normal children	1	2	A surpasses B in both environments but
school performance	B mental defectives	4	3	X is better for A and Y is better for B

		X England	Y West Africa	
races and	A Englishmen	1	4	A surpasses B in X
length of life	B West Africans	3	2	B surpasses A in Y but X is better for A and Y is better for B

mastiffs and dachshunds, living either on a good diet or on a starvation diet. Each race of dog will be heavier on the better diet but in either environment the mastiffs would be heavier than the dachshunds. For a second kind of situation Haldane compares Jersey cattle and Highland cattle, either on an English meadow or a Scottish moor. Although both sorts of cow will give more milk in England, with the Jersey cattle far surpassing the Highland cattle, on the Scottish moor the Highland cattle will give more milk than the Jersey cattle. Thirdly, imagine normal children and mentally defective children, either in an ordinary school or in a special school for mental defectives. In both cases the normal children will do better but the environment that is better for the normal child will be worse for the defective child, and vice versa.

Haldane selected his last illustration before the recent period of medical progress and colonial independence. 'As an example of the fourth type let A be Englishmen and B West African negroes. Let X be an English town and Y the Gold Coast colony. Let the four populations be placed in order of their average lengths of life. We should probably find that the order was: English in England, negroes in Africa, negroes in England, English in Africa.' He observed that almost all current theory was based on the view that the type of interaction described in his first example was universal. Perhaps the interaction between nature and nurture was of a simpler type in the determination of human intelligence than in that of the milk-yield of cattle or the seed-yield of wheat plants? 'Possibly', Haldane commented. 'But even a thorough-going materialist might well doubt this.' Few have heeded Haldane's cautions of nearly forty years ago, against such phrases as 'a good heredity', 'a good environment', or 'a superior race'.

Faced with these perplexities in the way of any general solution to the question of nature and nurture,

'Cultures may be training very different kinds of people, yet with each culture wanting the ones they produce.'

other researchers have tried to dispose of it by a second approach, that of generalising the issue into permanent vagueness. You assert, in this case, that obviously heredity and environment are both very important, but to ask which is more important in any particular aspect of behaviour is like asking which contributes more to the area of a field, its length or its breadth. This dismissive line of argument has served at times as a polemical antidote to extreme hereditarian or environmentalist views, but is unilluminating; as some scientists say, it is a 'cop out'.

The road to resolution

A third approach, which is now beginning in earnest to resolve the nature/nurture issue, involves openmindedness and attention to detail. You do not ask global questions or offer global answers – as we shall see, they do not exist. Instead you take specific, welldefined aspects of human behaviour in well-defined situations, and pose very specific questions that can give clear-cut answers. Some of these questions are basically genetic: for instance, what aspects of a person's temperament are subject to hereditary influences? Others are framed from an environmental starting point: if Africans do poorly at American tests of cognitive skill, is it not wise to examine the influence of the local culture on habits of thought before deciding that the Africans differ genetically in their powers of thought? Current studies in these questions will be described later in the chapter, but meanwhile here are some other examples.

The University of Hawaii is carrying out a large and elaborate study involving cognitive tests and other measurements in 3000 families of different ethnic origins. Hawaii has the advantage of a mixed population where different ethnic groups fall within much the same socio-economic range. A typical question posed is not 'Is one race brighter than another' but 'Is the structure of cognition in Euro-Americans and people of Japanese origin the same.' It would not be the same if, for instance, one group scored high in one kind of test and low in another kind of test, compared with the other group. In fact the result is null: there is no discernable difference in such respects between the Euro-Americans and Japanese-Americans.

Conspicuous differences show up, however, between people of different social status. Memory performance is a case in point, and here genetic differences seem to be relatively unimportant. This Hawaiian study, which at the time of writing has a couple of years to run, promises to be a definitive study of many aspects of heredity, environment and behaviour. Possible effects of mixed parenthood, left-handedness, age, sex and illness are being sought, and the safeguards go as far as checking that the weather has no effect on the test scores.

Human beings differ in their reaction to stress. Some people try to avoid stress, others enjoy the feeling generated by the hormones being released by stress and circulating in their blood. Some biologists now wonder whether there is an 'urban gene' – whether people who choose to live in big cities may differ genetically from those who prefer the quiet country life. Research in progress in Australia and Sweden will perhaps shed light on this question, which may be closely relevant to the diseases that doctors link with stress and chosen ways of life.

To shift to a case where environmental effects are more conspicuous, babies in the Netherlands develop more slowly than those in the United States. That is to say they run consistently behind the American babies in standard American tests of development, until the age of about two years. The differences between the

Polite Chinese infants. Both cultural and genetic explanations are on offer for the contrasts in behaviour between Chinese and American children.

ways Dutch and American mothers treat their babies seems reason enough. By tradition Dutch mothers wrap up their babies more tightly in their cribs, feed them at more precise intervals, give them fewer toys, and are generally afraid of 'spoiling' them.

The American tests inevitably reflect American norms of child behaviour. Babies are expected, for instance, to be active and always pursuing new experiences or different toys; the tests of 'exploration' in six-month-old babies are based on that assumption. To Dutch experts such behaviour represents a lack of ability to make creative use of a single toy. In describing her study of these differences, Freda Rebelsky of Boston University comments: 'Both cultures may be training very different kinds of people, yet with each culture wanting the ones they produce.'

The evidence about temperamental differences in different human populations is tantalising. The Chinese, for instance, have long been considered 'inscrutable' by Westerners. When a party of eminent American child psychologists returned from a visit to China one of them told me that the experience 'blew his mind'. The infants behaved quite differently from American infants: they were quieter, more polite, less aggressive and they sat still for long periods, to the amazement of the visitors. For an environmental explanation, one can look to the long Chinese traditions of quietude, self-effacement and concern about not losing face, and American traditions of self-assertion. One anthropological theory distinguishes between oriental 'shame' cultures, and Western 'guilt' cultures, according to the emotion evoked by social failures of various kinds. They affect the policies of individuals. But some biologists suspect that those cultural differences may reflect genetic differences in temperament.

The biologists point to three measurable contrasts. The Chinese, along with their near relatives the Japanese, Eskimos and American Indians, generally blush more readily than white people do. There is also less difference between Chinese men and women in stature and in some aspects of behaviour. And newborn babies of Chinese or related descent are quieter and more placid than white or black babies are. An environmentalist retort, on this last point, would be that Chinese mothers have learned to move about more carefully before the baby is born, and the baby is less agitated. But is it far-fetched to think that the dispersal of mankind to different environments resulted in shifts in temperament? Or to suppose that better understanding of influences on the behaviour of people in the world's largest nation might one day contribute to world peace? Although the arguments continue about possible temperamental biases in different populations, there need no longer be any doubt about a genetic factor in differences of temperament between individuals in the same population.

Easy and difficult children

In the 1950s a group of psychiatrists in New York developed a way of gathering objective information about differences in temperament in babies. Alexander Thomas, Stella Chess and Herbert Birch wanted to trace the origins of psychological problems in later life which affected children whose experiences and upbringing were not noticeably different from those of other children who remained problem-free. They wondered, too, why domineering parents made one youngster submissive, while another would become defiant. The child's individual style of responding to the environment, his temperament, would (they thought) help to determine how environmental influences affected him.

Thomas, Chess and Birch devised a way of assessing temperament from detailed descriptions of children's behaviour obtained in carefully planned interviews with their parents. An important aspect of the techniques is that parents are asked for factual information (does the child wriggle when being dressed?) rather than for vague opinions (is the child restless?). The reliability of the reporting can be checked by direct observation of the children, and it turns out to be good. The original group of 141 middle-class children, who first came under study at two or three months of age, is now entering adulthood. The children have been followed through infancy and schooling and some of the characteristics of temperament, identified in the cradle, have tended to persist. Other groups of children, including Puerto Ricans in New York, are also being studied as they grow up.

The analysis of temperament involves taking the parents' reports and scoring nine different characteristics, each on a three-point scale (high, medium and low). These characteristics are: level of activity; rhythmicity of eating, sleeping and excreting; distractability from ongoing activities; approach or withdrawal response to a new object or person; adaptability to changes in the environment; attention span, or persistence; intensity of reaction, regardless of its quality or direction; threshold of responsiveness, or sensitivity; and the general quality of mood – cheerful or tearful, friendly or unfriendly. The researchers found that sixty-five per cent of their original 141 babies could be assigned to one of three general 'types' of temperament which they called 'easy children', 'difficult children' and 'slow to warm up'.

Easy children were very regular in their habits, approached new objects or people rather than withdrawing from them, adapted readily to new environments and in mood were friendly and joyful. Some forty per cent of the children fell into this category, while ten per cent were difficult: they were the op-posite in all the characteristics mentioned and showed intense reactions such as loud crying and violent tantrums. Another fifteen per cent of the children were slow to warm up, and had a low level of activity, an initial but not lasting tendency to withdraw from new objects or people, and were rather mild in their reactions. That left about thirty-five per cent of children who showed a mixture of characteristics not fitting into any of the three main groups.

To give a little colour to these generalisations, and at the same time to elaborate on one of the more obscure characteristics, let me mention some of the examples of 'threshold of responsiveness' given by Thomas and his colleagues. A sensitive, low-threshold child, at the age of two months, stops sucking his bottle when another person approaches. At six months he may be seen hiding his head from a bright light. At five years he is noticing that his mother has a new dress; at ten he is fussing about getting the temperature of the water in a shower exactly right. In other words he is sensitive to what is going on around him. Another child, with a high threshold, is less sensitive. He may be unperturbed by loud noises at two months; at six months he is unmindful of the fact that his nappy is wet; at five he is stoical about injections; at ten he is eating any food that is put in front of him.

There is an interplay of temperament and environment. The tolerance or intolerance shown by parents and teachers to the idiosyncracies of children may have an important bearing on their development. Given the normal routines of life, temperamental characteristics may cease to be conspicuous; for example most children come to tolerate having a bath even if they have been fretful to begin with. A child who has been 'slow to warm up' may become very happy and outward-going if he stays in the same group of children at school for years on end. But change the circumstances and the old

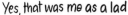

temperament may reassert itself. If the 'slow to warm up' child is suddenly transferred to another school he may go through an agonising period when he finds himself acting in a withdrawn and unfriendly fashion.

Most people, most of the time, manage to adjust their lives to suit their temperaments, and thereby camouflage them. And because so much depends on the events of the individual's life and how he copes with his temperament, the assessments made in infancy are not a reliable predictor of his characteristics as he grows older. Nevertheless the New York psychiatrists have found the assessments useful in a statistical sense for predicting which individuals may be at risk from mental illness. The 'difficult' children, in the original survey, showed a particularly high proportion with psychiatric problems by the age of ten.

But just how permanent a part of a person's constitution are these temperamental characteristics observed in infancy? Are they hereditary, written into the genes and therefore largely immutable in the person's biological makeup? One difficulty about these questions is that features of temperament showing at birth or shortly afterwards need not necessarily be genetic. The behaviour of a child in the first few months of life may be greatly affected by the circumstances of the pregnancy, the birth and early caretaking.

The question of which of the characteristics delineated by Thomas and his colleagues are really written into the genes, has been tackled in Norway, in a study instigated by Einar Kringlen, now at Oslo University, and Anne Mari Torgersen of Bergen University. It uses one of the human geneticists' favourite ploys: comparisons between twins. Characteristics of temperament that are inherited should be more alike in identical (monozygotic) twins, who come from a single fertilised egg, than in non-identical (dizygotic or fraternal) twins who come from different eggs, fertilised

independently, and therefore no more alike, genetically, than any other pair of brothers or sisters. Twin comparisons have been strongly criticised during the IQ controversy, on the grounds that identical twins are likely to be treated more alike, because they look alike. But in the first year of life this objection may not apply, as it is far from obvious, even to the mother, whether twins are identical or not.

Torgersen elected to study all pairs of twins of the same sex born in Bergen hospital during a year and nine months – more than fifty pairs altogether. She visited their homes when they were two months old and again when they were nine months old, for long interviews with their mothers using a questionnaire adapted from the New York study of temperament. After both visits each twin was separately scored for each of the nine characteristics of temperament. The scoring was done without knowledge of which pairs of twins were identical and which were not; this distinction was established independently by blood tests.

Torgersen finds that identical twins are more like each other in every one of the nine characteristics than are the two children in a non-identical pair. In every aspect, therefore, there seems to be a genetic factor at work. Between two months and nine months the identical twins become slightly more alike, while non-identical twins become conspicuously different in their temperaments. Presumably differences due to circumstances of birth are declining.

The consistency between identical twins is particularly striking in three characteristics. These are rhythmicity, approach versus withdrawal, and threshold of responsiveness; and are presumably most strongly determined by heredity. Some other characteristics, notably the children's mood (cheerful or tearful, friendly or unfriendly) and their attention span or persistence, are more variable and so more susceptible to environmental influences. The Norwegian study gives a strong biological underpinning to the New York psychiatrists' approach to individual personality by way of infant temperament.

Madness in the genes?

The victim of schizophrenia loses touch with reality and retreats into a fantastic, often anguished world existing only in his own head, where he pursues elaborate but meaningless trains of thought. Schizophrenia is the most widespread and persistent of the really serious mental illnesses and one person in a hundred becomes schizophrenic at some time in his life. As schizophrenia often strikes young adults and as many of its victims are confined to hospital for long periods, if not for life, large populations of patients arise from this one illness. For a hundred years or more psychiatrists have recognised that 'madness runs in families', although they have been divided into warring camps about the reasons.

On the one hand you can argue that the bizarre behaviour of one sick member of a family will create tensions that tend to drive others into mental illness; more generally, peculiarities of environment and behaviour persisting in a family can affect more than one member. Ronald Laing, for instance, thinks that making an individual feel excluded from the family circle can lead to schizophrenia. Other modern investigators offer to predict which families are 'risky' in the sense of being liable to cause a relapse in a schizophrenic patient released from hospital, and think they can advise such families how to treat him with proper consideration.

The other camp has affirmed with equal vehemence that schizophrenia is an actual bodily defect that deranges the brain and is transmitted by heredity.

From 1916 onwards a succession of investigations into family trees and comparisons of twins brought out seemingly strong evidence to this effect. A survey in New York State led to the conclusion that, if one member of a pair of identical twins was a schizophrenic, there was an eighty-five per cent chance of the other member being mentally sick too. The corresponding risk for non-identical twins was only fifteen per cent. Such figures implied a very strong genetic component in schizophrenia. Yet many psychiatrists remained unconvinced.

The issue of schizophrenia was a classic nature/nurture controversy, with both sides single-minded in their bodily or psychological interpretations of the causes of the disease. In the 1970s the matter may well have been resolved and in a manner that leaves both sides right in their basic claims and wrong in their obstinacy. Both genetic and environmental factors are very important and to ignore either of them is irresponsible.

Twins of Norway again supply the verdict, thanks to exceptionally thorough medical records maintained in that country. It was suspicion of the sampling methods used in earlier studies of the genetics of schizophrenia which led Einar Kringlen to make an ambitious study. In particular he thought there was a natural tendency in hospital staffs to remember cases where both twins of a pair were schizophrenic, and to forget or even fail to register cases where only one twin was sick. Kringlen, therefore, compiled an almost complete register of all the pairs of twins born in Norway in the first thirty years of this century. He then compared his list with national records of all psychiatric treatment in Norwegian hospitals since 1916. He was thus able to get an unbiased collection of the cases where one or both twins were schizophrenic. In hundreds of pairs only one twin was sick.

Remember the figure of eighty-five per cent mentioned earlier, for 'concordance' between identical twins. Kringlen finds, even after further psychiatric examination of the individuals concerned, that the chance of the second member of a pair of identical twins being schizophrenic, if the first is, comes out at only twenty-five per cent. That is using a strict definition of schizophrenia; by a looser interpretation of the mental condition, the figure is thirty-eight per cent. The risk is nevertheless three times greater than among non-identical twins, so there is no mistaking the genetic component predisposing a person to schizophrenia (unless one is to make a very great deal of the similar treatment accorded to similar-looking people). But the failure of the genetic factor to manifest itself as mental illness in twice as many contradictory cases points to the overriding importance of environmental factors that can either make a person demented or keep him healthy. Psychiatrists are, therefore, encouraged in their search for family circumstances and other factors that can conspire with latent genetic influences, in creating schizophrenia. Kringlen himself emphasises the importance of these environmental factors.

Yet the genetic component remains, so there is still encouragement for those researchers who want to pinpoint the bodily disorder involved. It probably involves a biochemical peculiarity, and more effective, 'tailor-made' drugs for treating schizophrenic patients might relieve a great deal of their suffering and greatly reduce the burden on the community that long-term care in mental hospitals represents. So, modern research resolves an old controversy in a clear way: in individual cases of schizophrenia psychiatrists are right to look for precipitating circumstances and to try to dissipate their effects, but if the eradication of schizophrenia is ever to be achieved then the brain researchers and geneticists will have to play their part.

Together, the psychiatrists and biologists have to specify precisely what is going on organically, precisely what is happening psychosocially, and precisely how the two processes interact.

After that appropriate division of labour, we turn to a quite different investigation, where the emphasis is wholly on cultural environmental factors. It bears closely, though, upon the issue of nature and nurture. Many people have been too quick to see explanations in racial genetics for apparent inability among people in other parts of the world to cope with simple problems, and too quick to attribute a primitive mentality to people living in primitive conditions.

Rice and reasoning

For five hundred years the Kpelle people have lived by growing rice in clearings in the tropical rain forest of West Africa. Tradition runs through their lives as strongly as malaria does. The secret societies, Poro for the men and Saude for the women, are in some senses more important then the public life of the villages. Every Kpelle adult has been through the initiation of the Bush school – requiring symbolic death in the forest and his later reappearance as an adult. Wisdom is equated with preventing changes in the precarious way of life in Kpelleland.

A highway now cuts through the Liberian rain forest, bringing traders and government officials. Teachers came, too, offering literacy to the Kpelle people. But Western-style mathematics, in particular, seemed to give the Kpelle children great problems. In 1964 two Americans, John Gay (a missionary and social scientist) and Michael Cole (a psychologist) set out to discover what the snags were. The research that they put in hand, and still continue in Liberia today, has classic qualities. It unites experimental psychology and

New roofs, new thoughts. For five centuries the Kpelle people of Liberia have cleared the African rain forest to grow their rice. Now that their isolation is ending, they turn out to think differently from Westerners.

An irregular world. John Gay will show the slide to the Kpelle boy for a split second and ask him how many dots there are on it. Random patterns like this one are scarcely more difficult for Kpelle children than regular patterns of dots – which American children find very much easier.

anthropology in an unprecedented fashion. It shows that human ability is in many respects not so much a property of a person as of his community and his way of life.

From their base at Cuttington College, a missionary centre, Gay and Cole and their Kpelle research assistants went into the nearby villages to discover the aptitudes of children and adults. They began with standard American tests. The Kpelle children encountered difficulties not experienced by their opposite numbers in the United States or Europe. Take, for instance, an American apparatus the experimenters used to test powers of reasoning.

The equipment resembles an automatic vending machine, operated by a ball-bearing and delivering a metal charm. By opening a flap and pressing a button to one side of the apparatus, the child can obtain a ball-bearing; another button behind another flap produces a marble, which does not work the charm-delivery system. Among third-grade (nine-year-old) American children to whom these features have been demonstrated, about half deduce immediately and correctly that they must find and push the right-hand button, get the ball-bearing, feed it into the middle hole and obtain the little reward. Very few Kpelle children do so. But then many of them are reluctant to press any button at all; they are likely to finger the case of the apparatus, looking perplexed.

As soon as anyone mentions it, it is obvious that vending machines, pushbuttons and steel balls are no part of the Kpelle way of life. The 'experimental anthropologists' tried the same test of reasoning with more familiar objects: a black key and red key, each in a matchbox, and a locked box which could be opened with (say) the red key. The problem of inference was exactly the same. Now, with the peculiarities of the apparatus no longer disabling them, the Kpelle children

performed, if anything, better than the American children who used the machine.

Other effects of cultural differences are harder to circumvent. Consider the test in which a child looks into an eyepiece and sees for a flash – less than a tenth of a second – a translucent sheet carrying a number of dots. He has to report how many there are. Sometimes the dots are scattered at random; sometimes they are arranged neatly in a geometric pattern, and for American children that makes a big difference. They can report up to six dots correctly and make sophisticated guesses beyond that, provided the dots are in a pattern. They do worse with a random arrangement, which is not easy for anyone to count in a quick flash. But African youngsters find the task just as difficult whether the dots are in a pattern or at random. The reason may be that the Kpelle child's everyday visual world has fewer comparable patterns in it: such as egg boxes, regular arrays of windows, and tidily stacked packets of food in the shops.

The tables can be turned. Cultural differences work in the Kpelle's favour in another test, the one most often quoted when the work of Gay and Cole is mentioned among their fellow scientists. The test consists of showing someone a bowl of uncooked rice and a measuring cup and asking him how many cupfuls of rice there are in the bowl. When there were in fact nine cupfuls, a group of Americans in training for service as teachers in Liberia made individual guesses of anything from six to twenty. The average of these guesses was an overestimate of thirty-five per cent. The same test given to a group of illiterate Kpelle adults produced an average underestimate of eight per cent. The explanation again is simple: the Kpelle live by rice and its measurement is an important part of their daily lives.

'That's not fair!' some readers are doubtless complaining. The unfairness is the very point, the only unusual thing about this case being the Americans showing up badly compared with the Africans. All tests or tasks conveyed from one way of life to another are likely to be unfair, but that has not prevented colonial officials or even some anthropologists from concluding that Africans and others have childlike minds, because of their unfamiliarity with the sophisticated ways and symbols of the white man.

As Michael Cole points out forcibly, anybody who has not absorbed the middle-class values of European or American schoolteachers and psychologists is likely to do badly in standard tests of intelligence. Yet the investigations in Liberia have shown that the people are not lacking in particular mental abilities – rather they apply their minds to situations quite different from those valued or accepted in Western middle-class culture. In some areas of life Kpelle people may be more acute, for example in their knowledge of nature and in their social relations. The problem for teachers who have to bridge the habits of thought of traditional and modern societies is not one of dealing with mental defectives but of evolving a different strategy. From his home base at New York's Rockefeller University, Cole is starting to apply the same investigative philosophy among the underprivileged blacks of Harlem.

Once notions of 'better' and 'worse', or 'advanced' and 'primitive', are set aside the way is clearer to finding out about the differences in how people think, and how they are related to general culture, to literacy and to other factors. Arabic literacy, for instance, tends to centre on reading the Koran and memorising long passages from it; accordingly, people literate in Arabic may have exceptionally well-trained memories. As a matter of history the growth of modern culture has gone hand in hand with literacy.

Many scholars have suspected that learning to read and write alters the very way people think and act, but sorting out the factors can be difficult. As most people learn to read and write in school, how do you distinguish the effects of literacy on ways of thought, from other effects of sitting in a classroom? There a child assimilates belief, values, attitudes and habits of formal learning, as well as knowledge. Cole has found a special opportunity in Liberia, among the Vai people, near neighbours of the Kpelle.

The Vai have their own script. It was invented about 140 years ago by Duwalu Bukele to enable his people to keep records and write letters. Several thousand Vai people use it in everyday life, but they do not learn it in school so that they are not 'contaminated' by the experience of school. Among the Vai people, Cole has begun a research programme which assesses an individual's level of skill in reading and writing; investigates whether he uses his literacy in westernised or traditional settings; and tests how he performs, compared with unlettered compatriots, in verbal, logical and classifying tasks thought likely to be affected by literacy.

Meanwhile Gay has become involved in problems of economic development among his beloved Kpelle. For years, international experts have been trying in vain to persuade the Kpelle farmers to adopt better varieties of rice. They scratch a subsistence in poor forest soil, with yields far below those achieved in other parts of the world. Gay has uncovered some of the reasons for the visiting experts' lack of success. Typically they would call on the male head of a household and explain the virtues of the improved seeds. The head of the household would be impressed by what he was told, and would pass on the good tidings, along with a supply of the seeds, to his wife. But instead of keeping the seeds for sowing the wife might well cook them and serve them for supper. What seems to be irresponsibility turns out to be entirely sensible in the Kpelle setting.

Rice expert. Among the Kpelle, the women are far more knowledgeable than the men about rice and its cultivation.

The experts made a cardinal mistake. They failed to realise that, among the Kpelle, the women are the authorities on rice. They are experienced plant breeders in their own right. At each harvest, the women select the best rice for next year's sowing. No self-respecting Kpelle woman would sow seeds from plants whose full-grown quality she had not verified with her own eyes. So the family might as well eat the seeds. The international authorities have been advised to change their approach to the improvement of Kpelle agriculture.

Gay has a simple test that brings out the difference between Kpelle men and women in their knowledge of rice. Two people sit back to back; in front of each of them is the same assortment of ears of different varieties of rice. One person has to pick up an ear and describe it so that the other can pick it out from among the other varieties. Two men find this task almost impossible to accomplish; the one offers hopelessly vague descriptions, the other optimistically guesses – usually wrongly. But two Kpelle women will do it very easily and briskly, with few errors.

Deprivation at White Dust

Short of hitting him repeatedly on the head, to deprive him of proper food might seem the worst possible insult to a developing human being. And if you want action that will put a stop to famines, and to the less severe but more prolonged malnutrition suffered by untold millions of people, you may be tempted to seize upon the evidence that malnutrition produces measurable delays in the development of children. If, on the other hand, you are concerned about better educational opportunities for the world's poor, you may want to play down any such findings. Miserly people might write off the children as not worth educating. Others

again fear neo-racists ascribing a supposed general stupidity to the world's poorest nations, due to bad feeding. These political cross-currents about 'deficits' and 'remediability' sweep through what is already murky water, because discovering the effects of hunger on the mental functions is technically difficult. After many years of research and controversy about this basic part of human nurture, the conclusions that are surfacing include new and subtle elements.

Bodily mechanisms for 'sparing' the brain are among nature's defences against the worst effects of hunger on the growing human organism. As a starving child wastes away, the brain is the last part of his body to suffer. Some doctors think that a child will die before irreparable damage occurs in his central nervous system – physical deterioration, that is to say, which cannot be made good by later growth. A theoretical argument says that the brain is so important for human beings that our evolution, which must have accompanied our ancestors through many episodes of hunger, arrived at procedures for maintaining the brain in working order, even in a stunted body. If undernourishment halts or even reverses the brain's growth, it can nevertheless resume as normal, although a little tardily, whenever food supplies improve.

Controlled experiments in human adversity fortunately cannot be performed by scientists. But the German army carried one out in the Netherlands in the winter of 1944–5, by stopping all transport of food. As a result there was terrible starvation, especially in the cities, until the liberation. Pregnant women and their babies were among the sufferers, birth weights were markedly reduced and many babies must have suffered corresponding setbacks in their brain growth at a critical period. When the male babies grew up and were conscripted, the military authorities assessed their physique and mental capacities. Many years later, scientists quarried the hospital records of 1945 and the later military records. A thorough study, published in 1975, had encouraging conclusions. No long-term effects of damage to body or brain could be discovered in the starvation victims. Nevertheless, the Dutch experience of short, sharp starvation, grievous though it was, may not be typical of the problem in other countries where a child may be malnourished for years on end.

In the mid-1960s Joaquin Cravioto, a pediatrician, of Mexico City, had suspected that there might be lifelong mental deficits in children who were severely malnourished during the first six months of their lives. Ten years later Cravioto had recast his ideas into a wider framework. He now accepts that physical restoration of the malnourished brain occurs, and that, given the right social opportunities, the deprived child can, in principle, catch up with his more fortunate peers by adulthood. But he argues that competitive societies often deny the child that opportunity, by branding him as backward according to his chronological age.

Since 1966 Cravioto and a team of doctors, nutritionists, psychologists and social scientists have been carrying out a thorough study of the effects of malnutrition in the semi-tropical farming country of central Mexico. The area is vulnerable to droughts that bring hunger and hardship and although malnutrition is usually moderate it may persist indefinitely. Cravioto selected a village and adopted an unofficial name to preserve its privacy: 'Land of White Dust'. The team was represented at the birth of every child born in the village during a period of twelve months, about 300 altogether. The condition of the mother and the child at the time of the birth is an important factor for any study of childhood. Since then the physical and psychological progress of the children has been followed closely.

The team monitors many of the factors of village life that may be affecting the children, for instance they assess the emotional as well as the material qualities of life in each household. They find that the houses themselves are reliable indicators of the family's financial status. Psychological tests administered once a month show that poorly fed children perform poorly by the standard measures of mental skill. But there are emotional factors, too. For example deprived children are more likely to think of their parents as being generally unhappy. Tested with a picture of an angry face, and asked to say how they would request the return of a ball from a man looking like that, deprived children are less likely to realise that they need to be especially polite to an angry man. In other words, something is going wrong with the children's social skills. Indeed their poor performance in intellectual tasks may be due not to want of intelligence but to a lack of persistence, or unwillingness to cooperate with the tester. The child may make excuses for not trying a task, or attempt to change the subject.

Food is not just a matter of nourishment – that is the thrust of Cravioto's present line of reasoning. For a small child, the smell and texture of different foods are an important part of his exploration of the world. And at the family table the child really begins to learn about the culture into which he has been born. He sees a microcosm of social interactions, in the roles played by the father, the mother and older brothers and sisters. Even learning which menus are appropriate to each meal is, according to some anthropologists, a very profound and symbolic part of culture. Strip the table of food, in hard times, and the child falls behind in his social education.

Few sights are more disquieting than a grossly malnourished child. The twig-like limbs are not so dreadful to behold as the withdrawn and listless expression of an

infant who seems to be concentrating entirely on keeping still and staying alive. People who have tried to force such a child to respond to his surroundings have found that doing so can throw him into convulsions. Among the acutely malnourished children in Mexico, the fortunate ones finish up at a children's hospital in Mexico City, under the care of Cravioto and his staff. In these emergency cases, too, Cravioto finds that malnutrition is not just a matter of food.

When hunger has applied the brakes to a child's mental and social development, as well as to his bodily growth, recovery from hunger is slow even in the best

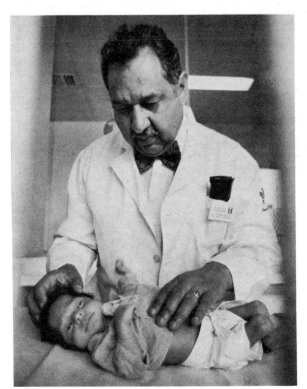

Rescue for a starved baby. Joaquin Cravioto at the IMAN Children's Hospital in Mexico City.

hospital conditions. In Cravioto's opinion, something better than the best is needed. A child needs nourishment for his emotions and interests as well as for his belly. Especially, he needs loving attention from adults. In an effort to prove that better care will make the children lose their apathy more quickly and gain weight more rapidly, Cravioto has established an experimental ward in the Mexico City hospital, with twice the normal staff. In a village not far from 'White Dust' he is trying out the same idea in rural conditions, in new investigations designed to see whether children who have plenty of mental stimulation during the first year of life are better able to resist the effects of malnutrition.

Malnutrition is certainly not the only cause of hindered growth in the intellectual and social skills of children. Illness, injury, neglect and emotional stress can all result in performance running behind that of other children. Provided the cause of the trouble is removed, the growing human being shows remarkable resilience. The deprived infant can grow up into lively adolescence and vigorous adulthood. But during the formative years he may be lagging, in stature and competence, behind other children of the same age. In primitive communities where calendars and stopwatches do not provide the measures of human worth, the consequences of a lag may be trivial. More advanced societies, obsessed with norms and the classification of individuals, may add to the injury of malnourishment or disease the insult of being branded as a second-class citizen.

The vision of the Crees

Injury or disease can plainly alter a person's behaviour in gross ways; for example, a bullet in the left side of the brain can rob a man of his powers of speech. But now it seems that experience can reach deep into the

human organism and leave its mark in much less obvious ways. The most remarkable report to this effect came in 1973. It concerned the Cree Indians of James Bay, Quebec, who had lived during their childhood in the traditional tepees, conical houses quite different from the box-shaped rooms in which most Westerners spend their early lives. Many of the Cree Indians are now resettled in conventional housing. But their visual perception differs in measurable ways from that of the 'Euro-Canadians'.

The background to this research was the knowledge that individual cells in the visual areas of the brain are allocated to detecting lines of particular slopes. The men responsible for the discovery, David Hubel and Torsten Wiesel of the Harvard Medical School, also found that the brains of kittens needed visual experience during the early weeks of their lives for the system of detectors to develop normally. Thereafter, other experiments in the United States, Canada and Britain provided for kittens to see only a world of stripes. They might be horizontal, vertical or sloping, but each animal saw stripes in just one orientation. As a result the brain cells appropriate to that orientation developed normally, but other cells did not.

In one test Donald Mitchell and his colleagues in Halifax, Nova Scotia, reared a kitten in this fashion and then sent the animal to a laboratory in California, without disclosing the slope of the lines to which the animal had been exposed. The other scientists correctly deduced the slope by measuring the responses of the kitten's brain cells to the sight of lines of various orientations.

In Halifax, Mitchell has been particularly concerned with comparable effects in human beings born with various eye defects. Astigmatism is a distortion in the lens of the eye which produces differing clarity of vision for slopes at different angles. As a result the

brain may not gain necessary experience in seeing lines at certain angles as sharply as it normally would. Appropriate spectacles can easily correct the focusing defect but if the remedy comes too late in life the brain may not recover its acuity of vision at certain angles. Squinting is another case in point; unless it is corrected early the brain may fail to learn how to develop its full powers in employing both eyes together – for example, in judging distances by stereoscopic means, using the slightly different views of the scene from the two eyes.

The word has gone out to the medical profession, to correct defects of vision early in life in case lasting damage is done. But what does 'early' mean? There have been conflicting reports about the age at which the human brain loses its ability to recuperate from early visual deprivation. A recent study at the University of Minnesota, on recovery from the effects of early squinting, suggests that the most critical period for the development of the visual system is at the age of eighteen months to two years; the opportunity for developing or recovering normal vision using both eyes together is falling off by about six years of age.

Even without eye defects, there are biases in the visual system of the brain. If you look at gratings at various angles and increasing distances (see page 96) a sloping grating becomes blurred first, while upright or horizontal gratings can be seen clearly at greater distances – perhaps as much as ten per cent further, which is not a trivial difference. The occurrence of sharpest vision with upright and horizontal gratings is normal, at any rate in people reared in conventional modern housing. But the Cree Indians of northern Canada who spent their infancy in and among conical tents were not surrounded by the same sights. Of course, they saw the natural horizon and tree trunks growing upright, but not the pervasive vertical and horizontal lines of buildings.

Seeing the world differently. Barrie Frost (standing) has found that Hugo Georgekish and others who grew up among the traditional dwellings of the Cree Indians do not show the commonplace bias in visual acuity for horizontal and vertical lines, which occurs even in newborn babies. You can test for this bias in yourself by observing the patterns on the left, with the eyes at a gradually increased distance from the page. You will probably find that the sloping lines become blurred first.

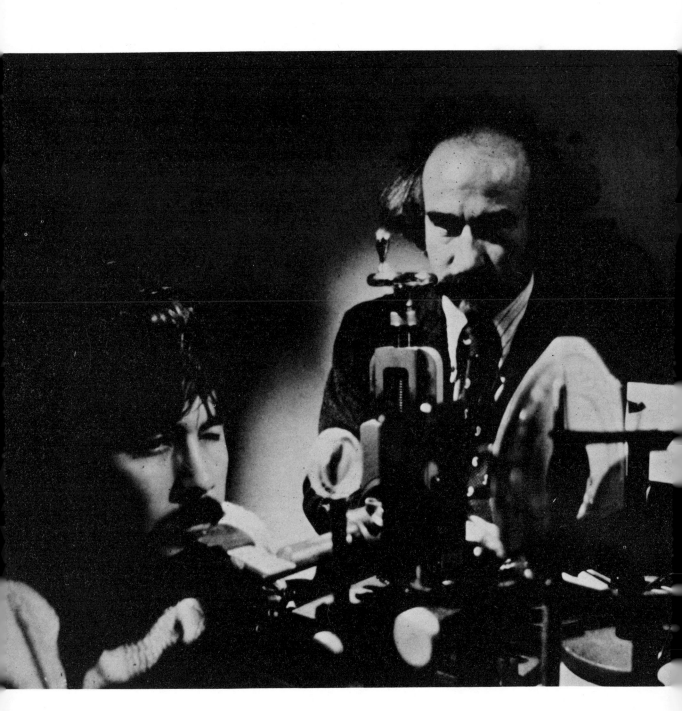

White man speak
with slanted tongue

In tests carried out at James Bay, a simple portable apparatus measured the visual acuity for horizontal, vertical and sloping lines. Sixteen Cree Indians were asked in turn to set a pointer parallel to the lines of a grating that they saw for only a few seconds. The distance of the grating gradually increased. Robert Annis and Barrie Frost, from Queen's University, Kingston, reported that these tests showed only slight differences in acuity, not statistically significant, according to the orientation of the grating, while the same tests in twenty Euro-Canadian students at Queen's University showed the usual sharper acuity for vertical and horizontal lines. While they could not rule out a possible genetic difference between the two groups, affecting the visual system, Annis and Frost argued that the simplest explanation was the difference in their visual experience in early life.

Some scepticism greeted this report. Experts criticised the simple procedures and variable lighting conditions in the testing at James Bay. But the implications for the effects of experience on brain function were far-reaching, and many scientists were eager for confirmation. In May 1975, Frost took a Cree Indian student from Queen's University, Hugo Georgekish, along to Dalhousie University in Halifax for tests with Donald Mitchell's more refined apparatus.

Physicists often make a pattern of light and dark stripes, equivalent to a grating, by letting light from a long narrow slit reach a screen by two different routes, so that the two sets of light-waves interfere with each other to produce the pattern of stripes. Mitchell used this principle, and a laser beam, to form a 'grating' directly on the retina of Hugo's eye. By this means he circumvented any irrelevant peculiarities of the Cree's vision, and it was a straightforward matter to vary the spacing and orientation of the lines formed on the retina. The results were favourable. That is to say,

Mitchell's tests confirmed an absence of the normal bias in favour of horizontal and vertical lines, in Hugo's visual acuity. The orientation made very little difference to his perception.

A controversy among the experts about the mechanisms runs through all investigations of the effects of early experience on vision. Some say that the cells of the brain are prewired to perform correctly, but that they need the stimulus of experience to confirm their functions; in other words, with disuse their powers may atrophy. Other scientists contend that, on the contrary, an active growth of connections between brain cells is required before they function properly, and that growth is promoted by use. This is not a narrowly technical issue: it bears upon general questions about how, and to what extent, experience can modify biology of the organism – not just in vision but in many other interactions of heredity and environment. Prewiring implies a stronger influence of genetic design; growth by stimulation makes the environment correspondingly more influential. At present this controversy is unresolved, but to say so does not detract from the importance of the experimental findings, which indicate that something profound and long-lasting is going on.

The evidence is clear, in kittens and in humans born with eye defects, that experience in infancy can affect a very basic part of the brain's operation, in many cases for life. It concerns a function that few people would previously have imagined to be so vulnerable to environmental influences. Chapter Two mentioned the plausible theory that the human being loses some of his power to distinguish speech sounds as he grows older, if he does not hear all of the sounds in his native language. Now the Canadian researches show that a Cree Indian who has grown up in traditional surroundings literally sees the world a little differently from the way you and I see it.

In place of dogma

Very different kinds of answers about nature and nurture come from the different studies I have detailed – a conclusion that is fully in keeping with the non-dogmatic approach commended at the outset of this chapter. First there were two areas where Norwegian research has explored the genetic factors at work. One was temperament, a plain case of genetic influences. People may be very skilful at adapting their lives and thereby making their individuality in this respect less obtrusive, but in times of stress the temperament in the genes may reassert itself. The schizophrenics, in the second example, seem to fit into much the same picture. Although a genetic factor is ultimately responsible for schizophrenia, most people inheriting it are able to lead essentially normal lives; certain kinds of environmental stress seem necessary to evoke the illness.

Then we set aside genetic factors and saw, among the people of Liberia, how the prevailing culture can markedly affect the way in which individuals think, making them proficient in tasks that are relevant to their way of life, and not necessarily to foreign intelligence tests. Pursuing another environmental influence, the studies in Mexico were beginning to put more emphasis on psychological and social factors during malnutrition and its aftermath, rather than on the direct effects of hunger on to the brain. But now, with the astigmatism of the Cree Indians of Canada, comes a remarkable inversion, in which environmental factors turn out to be affecting the visual system of the brain, which even the most ardent environmentalist might have expected to be completely under genetic control.

So who wins – the geneticist or the environmentalist? Even to pose such a question should by now seem curiously old-fashioned. Each aspect of behaviour involves different kinds of interplay of genes and environ-ment, and resolves itself differently in detail. And about remediability, the possibility of making good any injurious effects of the environment, the answer is similarly variable. While malnourished children often seem to recover spontaneously, some people who have slipped over the edge into schizophrenia may be re-trievable only with difficulty, and some defects of vision may not be correctable at all. But one must go further and look to individual differences in remediabi-lity. Some people are more vulnerable than others to particular kinds of environmental insult; similarly their powers of recuperation may vary.

A cripple may never learn to high-jump yet may manage to walk – if he is given help. The same reasoning applies to people thought to be intellectually or emo-tionally lame. The nature/nurture argument was never really symmetrical. Except in the fantasies of the eugenicists, a social group can exert little direct control on the genetic constitution of its members. But society has a strong influence on the circumstances of people's lives, and therefore responsibilities for their environ-ments. Even in extreme cases, where a known gene has drastic effects on behaviour, questions of environment and deprivation can recur. The hereditary disease called PKU, caused by a single gene, produces severe mental defects. But it can be treated by special diet and then the affected child will be normal. To deny such treatment, when the condition has been diagnosed, makes it a case of environmental deprivation for that child.

The resolution of the ancient issue of nature and nurture in terms of detailed knowledge may come to be counted one of the greatest achievements of twentieth-century science. The examples given represent, to be sure, only some important fragments of human behav-iour. An enormous amount remains to be discovered about the interplay of biology and culture, as it operates in the whole species, in different populations and in different individuals. Whole sectors of enquiry have been deliberately left aside in this treatment, such as the relationship between skin colour and the ecological history of populations, or the connection between belief systems and reproductive biology. In place of the absurd dogmatism of the recent past one now starts from the assumptions that biological and social factors interact in virtually every aspect of human life and that the mechanisms of interaction are likely to be different from case to case. The way ahead is then clear for significant and reliable discoveries, some of which we have sampled.

In the long run the old argument will seem like the squabbles among alchemists about the divine attributes of the elements. The interdependence of biological biases and social encouragement in the development of infants is so intimate that one cannot usefully regard the mother, for instance, as either an animal caretaker or as an agent deputed by society to mould the child. The two roles are thoroughly mixed up and compounded with the baby's manipulation of the mother; differences in the temperaments of babies and mothers ensure that the interaction will never be quite predictable.

In the perspective of evolution, too, nature and nurture become churned together. Human biological biases have influenced the character of society and the nurture it provides. Conversely, the character of society has influenced human evolution; yesterday's nurture becomes tomorrow's nature. The system would be intricate even if it related to unintelligent animals, even if the inventions and conscious decisions of the human conspiracy did not enter into it. But the complexity is not an excuse for reverting to a vague 'little-of-each' position and science is flexing new muscles for dealing with complex systems of this kind.

'What are you going to do with this knowledge when you have it?' The question was a political one and merits a political answer. Understanding nature and nurture will curb the more ridiculous propositions of the far right and far left. Genetic and environmental disadvantages suffered by individuals and groups will be mitigated with greater skill and effectiveness. Above all, the use of this research will be to sharpen our sense of wonder about the value to our species of having people of different genetic constitutions, and about the wide choice of social mechanisms for incorporating widely differing individuals into viable communities. Knowing more precisely why we are different may be the only way of preventing our differences from being forever a source of iniquity and war.

As to the issue about the 'malleability or incorrigibility' of people, and all that that implies for the quest for better ways of life, the mixed answers about nature and nurture coming out of current research confirm the general impressions of anthropology. Human beings are capable of making all kinds of societies, good or bad, and people behave appropriately within their culture. To that extent they are malleable. Yet in each community individuals vary enormously in temperament and other respects, which variations must in part be due to genetic differences. Unless some far-fetched eugenic programme is to be carried out, every imaginable society of the future will need to cater for human individuality and for the possibility of nonconformity. And to that many would say, thank goodness.

The culture of children endures across space and time. In England now they play the same game as Pieter Brueghel the Elder recorded in Holland more than four centuries ago.

4 : Complicity

Just behind our high foreheads are the so-called frontal lobes, relatively larger in man than in any other animal. The more advanced of the hominids of three million years ago had a brain little more than half the size of ours but, even in them, the high forehead is striking. The frontal lobes are not directly involved in interpreting the outside world or in moving muscles, but they make a profound contribution to our human nature. Their work includes planning and monitoring our actions. Ropes of nerves also connect the frontal lobes to the central parts of the brain concerned with emotion and bodily feeling. They seem to bring massive brain-power into play for monitoring and modifying our emotions; also for imagining emotions.

The man who says, 'I have a gut feeling it's the right thing to do,' may mean it almost literally. If you feel embarrassed in anticipation of a difficult interview, or joyful at the thought of meeting a friend, this interconnection of planning and emotion is probably involved. You can imagine in advance somebody's anger, and how you would feel about it, if you were to pursue a tempting but provocative course of action; so you may think better of it. Although there is not much direct proof, the nerve connections in question are plausibly key contributors to our social sensibility, and to our human capacity for anticipating how other people will react to our behaviour.

Culture of childhood

To gain new perspectives on human social behaviour, an anthropologist may travel far, facing hardship and disease, and may spend months or years slowly penetrating the mysteries of strange tribesmen who speak a parochial language. But there is one society, strikingly different from our own, whose members are virtually unarmed, reasonably friendly and guaranteed to be able to speak one's own language. No perilous or costly expedition is involved in finding them. You only have to step outside your door and you may glimpse one of them hiding behind a dustbin, while another runs screeching down the street as if all the devils of hell were after him. And on a fine summer evening you may chance upon a small group of them standing in solemn concourse while one of their number points at the others in turn and repeats a magical incantation. In England in the 1970s it might be:

Ibble, obble, black bobble,
Ibble, obble – out!

Between the ages of about six and twelve, the children of industrialised countries form distinct and half-secret communities of their own. They are at the zenith of childhood; they are neither incompetent infants nor aspirant adults, and childish affairs are important in their own right. Their communities flourish particularly well in the side-streets of towns, where children abound and traffic does not. The micro-landscape has useful features, such as a street lamp that can represent a home base, and doorways and alleys where a person can conceal himself. Iona and Peter Opie, the best-known collectors of childish folklore, regret the well-intended marshalling of children into fenced-off play-grounds. Such places are typically featureless and leave nowhere to hide. Children are accustomed to fixing their own tribal boundaries, so the fence is like an artificial frontier drawn by a colonial power. Play becomes less subtle and more aggressive in such confined places.

Just as many Europeans once credited fables that spoke of distant people who wore their faces in their chests, so adults today perpetuate extraordinary slanders about their own children. 'Oh they don't know any games, I'm afraid,' or 'Television has killed all the fun of childhood, you know,' are common remarks. They can be refuted by consulting the nearest eight-year-old native, listing his (or, better, her) repertoire of a dozen or more formal games and noting when the informant last played each of them. The adult investigator may dimly recall all of the games from his own childhood. The details and jargon vary from place to place and century to century, but most of the basic games are very old and very widespread. For instance, the game in which children hide and then have to run 'home' without being caught was known to the ancient Greeks as Apodidraskinda. Yet a young reporter may say in all sincerity: 'Mary made that one up.'

Games were not always peculiar to children. Just a couple of centuries ago, adults and children in Europe regularly chased and danced together, while 'nursery' rhymes and 'fairy' stories were a part of their shared culture. In many agrarian and hunting communities, adults and children still play the old games together. The rift between adults and children is tantamount to the invention of children as a separate, somewhat demeaned and stigmatised race of people. The notion that children needed special clothes, books and food crystallised in Europe in the eighteenth century.

Children's games and rituals give a fascinating insight into how human beings organise themselves in the absence of economic constraints or any clearly defined political power. The important thing is a set of rules and procedures, known to all, which govern joint activities and cope efficiently with conflicts that arise. Children have to be willing to learn the rules, which are strictly traditional for the place in question, and cannot ordinarily be improvised. Sometimes one will see, just outside a group, other children closely attending to what is going on. They are likely to be newcomers to the district, studying unfamiliar procedures, learning unfamiliar rhymes. Newcomers rarely presume to import the games and rituals of their former home. A child whose classroom performance is the despair of his

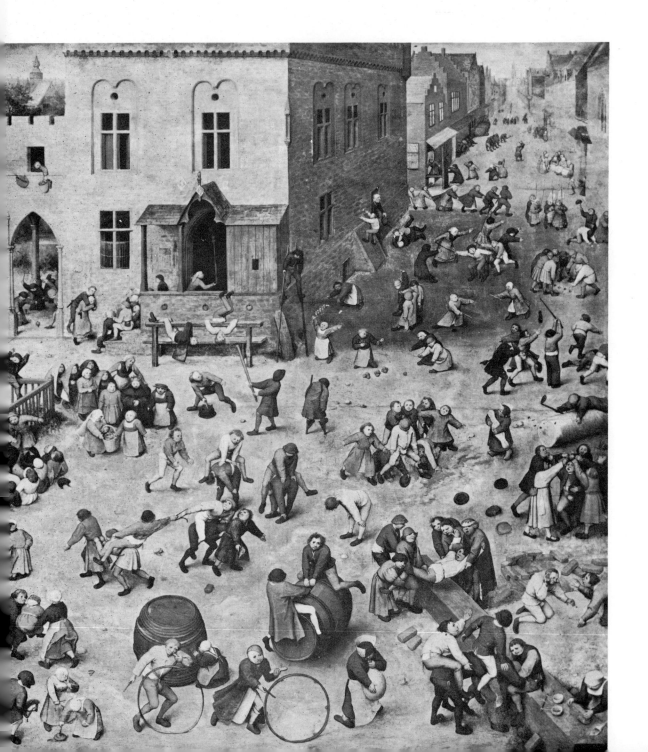

teachers may show great aptitude and powers of memory for the unwritten culture of his street.

A socially sophisticated child needs to know a lot. He should be wary of mock riddles of this kind:

Adam and Eve and Pinch-me
Went down to the river to bathe.
Adam and Eve were drowned.
Who do you think was saved?

– because the logical answer, 'pinch-me', brings disagreeable consequences. There are also superstitions which the child can take as seriously as he wishes. English examples collected by the Opies include avoiding walking on the lines between paving stones and fear of cross-eyed women, while ladybirds or touching a sailor's collar are among the many objects thought to bring good luck. For two children to say the same thing at once, by accident, may appear to them a very fateful event, to be followed by linking little fingers, naming a famous writer (Shakespeare in London, Goethe in Hamburg) and making a wish.

For maintaining public order in the childish community there are special words, phrases and procedures. A found object can be claimed irrevocably by the child who is first to utter the right formula, 'bags' for example. The childish habit of making gifts or exchanges and then regretting them is kept in check by ritual procedures such as linking fingers and saying:

Touch teeth, touch leather,
No backsies for ever and ever.

Similarly doubts about the truthfulness of a statement can be dispelled by a serious oath; for instance:

My finger's wet
My finger's dry
Cut my throat if I tell a lie.

It often happens in the course of a game or contest or even a fight that a child needs to rest or recuperate for a moment and there is a formula for that, too ('fay-nights' or 'scribs' in southern England) which another child is bound to respect, and not regard in any way as a sign of surrender. Children may resolve disputes with little duels of their own, but the overall authority of the community can vent itself on a child judged to have acted dishonourably, when the other children group themselves around the offender and chant an alarming and humiliating jeer: 'cowardy cowardy custard . . .', 'cry baby cry . . .' or 'tell tale tit, your tongue shall be slit . . .'.

An adult should hesitate before labelling any particular action of a child – for example 'bagging' an object – as unfair or reprehensible, just as an anthropologist must be cautious about condemning strange practices in a savage tribe. What matters is the overall functioning of the community and the welfare of individuals, and in these respects the children appear very civilised and sensible. In the children's world there are no scores, no prizes, no umpires. Priest-like figures have especially full knowledge of the oral traditions, but within the games no one is considered better than anyone else; real competition is minimised.

What the observation of children tells us most clearly about our human nature is our ready conformity to the behaviour of the majority. Children are eager to learn the social rules, and equally ready to teach and counsel one another. Besides the games and rituals peculiar to their culture children also, of course, play adult games like football and they engage in free-ranging play, such as cowboys and indians, or doctors and nurses, in which they act out roles. Children frequently feign sudden death. They also practise control of their bodies (in 'statues', for instance) and of their facial expressions (blushes and laughter). All of these skills, including knowing how to lie with a straight face, come in handy in the less innocent worlds of adolescence and adulthood. But children are happily unaware of their games being any kind of preparation for anything; their world is complete in itself.

Social sensibility

To observe human beings dispassionately in any real social setting is difficult. The observer is liable to become interested in the business in hand or in personal feelings about the individuals present. Movie cameras and tape recorders give more faithful records, but awareness that these modern aids are being used will alter people's behaviour; while a hidden 'candid camera' involves ethical problems for the sensitive investigator.

Many playwrights, novelists and film-makers have won lasting distinction by their ability to produce versions of human interactions which, while highly edited and over-eloquent, nevertheless capture recognisable methods, tensions and nuances in human interactions. That Aristophanes or Chaplin can be applauded in cultures far removed from their own in space and time suggests they have indeed identified some universals in human social behaviour. Far fewer philosophers and scientists have been as successful in dealing with the events of everyday life.

Exceptions stand out. Niccolo Machiavelli blackened his name by his shrewd, seemingly amoral assessment of villainous techniques to which men who would win political power could have resort. He drew on history and on his own experiences as a diplomat of Florence around the start of the sixteenth century. At that time, too, Erasmus of Rotterdam was drawing parallels between human life and a stage play. In our own century, C. H. Cooley and G. H. Mead in the United States and Jean-Paul Sartre in France have emphasised the symbolic nature of human interactions and the concern of participants about the impressions they are making on one another. And recently the students of animal behaviour and their imitators have begun to apply to humans the skills acquired in observing animals dispassionately, bringing new knowledge about gestures, facial expressions and courtesies of human beings in interaction.

The man who in our time quarries from commonplace situations the richest lodes of human behaviour is Erving Goffman of the University of Pennsylvania. In a long succession of essays on what people actually do in face-to-face situations of many kinds, he has carried forward a tradition in social science whereby individuals in a social setting are seen to be playing roles more or less as actors do. Each appears to be making a display, to promote an impression of his character, social status and intentions. Newspaper reports or novels are as likely to supply Goffman with instances of behaviour as are the learned studies on which he also draws freely; hence one reads about James Bond or sword swallowers or the husband who takes his secretary to the Virgin Islands. But careful observation transforms questions of etiquette into microsociology.

Goffman perceives marks of human social sensibility among, for example, pedestrians who navigate a crowded pavement without colliding. From the research of Ralph Birdwhistell, he describes how each person scans an oval of space ahead of him, watching for intruders into the space who may make manoeuvring necessary. Action taken in good time avoids loss of dignity. Unthinkingly each person signals his intentions with his body. A slight twist to the trunk, for instance turning the shoulder forward, can indicate the side on which the person proposes to pass, while he makes a very small sidestep in the same direction. The other person reciprocates the signal and mutual glances, involving subtle recognition, help to ensure that signals have been exchanged. But when the people have be-

The 6.15 train to Dogsbury will depart from platform 4

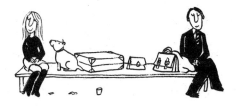

come closer, perhaps eight feet apart, they turn their eyes downwards lest they seem too inquisitive. When the path is too narrow for passing, one party may signal to the other to come on first. But he may do it in a mocking way that implies no real subordination. The other will acknowledge as much, by making mock gestures of hurrying.

People are jealous of the personal space around them and are also careful not to seem to intrude on the spaces of others. Strangers will not willingly crowd together, but if there is only one seat left in a row a person can take it, even if that means sitting close to an attractive member of the opposite sex. But a tricky problem can arise if everyone else then leaves. Two strangers sitting close together find that they are unexpectedly signalling a relationship, as if they are either with each other or interested in each other. But to move away ungraciously might imply a repulsion such as body smell. So a further signal may be necessary, to suggest that the only purpose in moving away is to give more room.

Human beings lay temporary claim to pieces of the Earth's surface, for example by leaving a coat on a seat. Lines of gaze can also be claimed, so that you may be careful to avoid walking between a person and something he is looking at. One person can intrude on another's privacy simply by staring, but he may be deterred by a return stare. These are some of the techniques of territory-control in human society. Goffman likens them to the claims to territory made by other animals, although human behaviour in this respect is far more delicate.

An encounter between humans typically begins with one person catching the eye of another. If the attempt is rebuffed the initiator can pretend that he did not really mean it, but the other person may signal with his eyes, voice or stance that he is available. Once a conversation between two or more people is in progress,

there is usually teamwork – an unspoken conspiracy that allows each person to carry off the role he seems to have chosen. Should one of them show signs of slipping in his performance, the others will give him warning hints. If someone is telling an incredible tall story about himself, they may look at him quizzically or exchange a sceptical glance. The offender then adjusts his performance to save face, perhaps by pretending he was only joking. Each person sees himself through the eyes of the others, and social encounters are rituals in which participants regulate their own behaviour – each trying to protect and sustain the impression of his own worth and the worth of the others present.

Stepping out of frame

When Erving Goffman applies the term 'reality' to a game of chess, he knows what he is doing. Consider two adults playing chess for fun. Besides the game itself a gaming encounter is in progress. The players are absorbed in the game, attending to rules and actions of a generally abstract quality. They are unconcerned about any hubbub around them, scarcely noticing even the quality of the pieces or the board. If a piece accidentally falls off the board, they will recover it absent-mindedly; the action is an irrelevancy. Thus, apart from the rules of chess, there are rules for the management of engrossment, for sorting out what is relevant and irrelevant.

The human brain functions, and has to function, in this way, deciding what signals and events it should focus upon, and what ignore. In his engrossment, a person tends even to lose sight of the fact that he is engrossed. Being engrossed is to a degree 'psychobiological' and unintentional, in a way that pretending to be engrossed is not. In the social context, correctly maintaining the engrossment is crucial for each player's sense of identity and mutual respect – in fact for his

sense of reality. But break the social rules, introduce an irrelevancy that cannot be ignored, as when one of the players makes a gesture of boredom, and the game loses its immediate reality, the spell is broken. The human sense of reality, of being at ease with the world, depends on flimsy rules of courtesy and etiquette – not just in games of chess but in all encounters between human beings.

Psychotics and comics habitually break the social rules and thus dispel reality. Goffman also contrasts the usual policy of putting others at their ease with police interrogations which set out to discomfit the suspect. The aim is to make him lose his self-control and therefore unable to preserve a feigned impression. Spies and counter-spies provide rich material for Goffman, because among them the human ability to act a false part is exploited, perverted and played with in all kinds of devious ways. Naturally, Goffman is less concerned with the problems of the CIA than with the general lesson, that agents are a little like us all and all of us a little like agents. 'There is no one . . . who has not fabricated a ''good'' reason for actions that spring from a concealed intent.'

For the television programme of *The Human Conspiracy*, we thought of illustrating Goffman's observations of the human scene by using actors to depict little interactional vignettes. Now, in his latest study, *Frame Analysis*, Goffman deals with the conventions and deceptions that define a social situation, and these include theatrical and other presentations. It is salutary for the script-writer to note how Goffman's use of analysis would apply, even in barest outline, to this treatment of Goffman's own work.

What the viewers at home see is not 'coverage' of live events, but a scripted version of events mocked up for the avowed purpose of illustration. But illustrations, even if frankly presented as such, are not perfectly

innocent. They succeed only to the degree that the skill of their staging causes viewers to fall into somehow treating the events as though they were real, when in fact the viewers know they are not. The performers act as if they do not know what is about to unfold, yet they do know because they rehearsed each scene. Any obvious sign that mere acting is going on is displeasing to the audience, which wants to be convinced of the naturalness of what it sees. That demands from the actors a profound insincerity which, paradoxically, will earn them the credit of being sincere.

The very concept of a documentary programme as a mirror of reality is suspect. Film of scientists at work often encourages an impression of eavesdropping on real events when in practice it is staged, with the scientists willingly mimicking themselves. Much selection and editing are involved and there is a built-in bias in favour of what happens to be succinctly expressable. Thus the impression given of Goffman's work, for example, is at best only a sampling that happens to fit the format and time available, and the rather arbitrary shape of a programme called *The Human Conspiracy*. Matters of only specialist interest do not appear, nor the footnotes wherein Goffman credits other researchers whose work he draws upon. But to admit this during the transmission of the programme would itself be suspect, for it might be intended to strengthen the trust the viewer has in the fairmindedness of the producer.

Goffman's own method of research is a frame. He calls it 'role distance', mentally standing back from social interactions and observing them sceptically. Role distance is both the scientific method of the observer and an important part of what he sees other people doing. Analyst and participant are both searching for rules that govern proper behaviour, and the rules are often similar to those adopted in formal rituals and in games played for fun. In well-defined social roles, such as nurse or policeman or boss, the 'front' to be adopted is often established in advance. But a person may play quite different roles in different social settings. A human being is normally adept at adjusting his behaviour to the situation because he sees himself through the eyes of others. There is no saying which is the real person, and his capacity for role distance heightens the uncertainty.

A person may step out of frame, by making a joke or otherwise distancing himself from the business in hand. The older child who fools about on a merry-go-round is dissociating himself from the role of rider that a four-year-old takes very seriously. Similarly a junior surgeon may be permitted the function of jester during a serious operation. The simulated bumbling of the Victorian gentleman-amateur sometimes concealed great skill. People seldom go through their appointed tasks like wooden soldiers; by role distance an individual expresses his personal style. It helps to give an impression of being a nice, well-rounded person.

So behind the role that an individual is adopting there will be hints of something else. As Goffman says, '. . . something will glitter or smoulder or otherwise make itself apparent beyond the covering that is officially worn.' This seems to be the real self, the personality peeping through. But for Goffman it is no more real, no less illusory, than the outward role itself. Providing a *sense* of what sort of person he might be behind the role he is in is part of the game; he may do the same sort of thing in any situation but the hints he gives of his 'self' in different settings may have little in common with one another. In Goffman's words: 'The individual, bringing together in various ways all the connections he has in life, becomes a blur.'

Goffman's analysis connects with biology at several points. Our brains, for instance, crave contact with other people. The great human capacity for social fore-sight allows us to rehearse the likely responses of others to various kinds of behaviour, to think out the game a few moves ahead, to see what behaviour may be unacceptable, to select the best strategy. The brain is wired for just such anticipation. And there is a human repertoire of effective social signals, akin to those that biologists see passing among other animals.

Sometimes the brain focuses on the business in hand in an unpretending, unselfconscious way. For fully engrossed chess players the game is more real than many of the serious pretences of everyday life. Proper involvement generates proper conduct. And although individuals differ in their social competency, no one can maintain a front beyond a certain point, without collapsing into embarrassment, fear or mirth – 'flooding out' as Goffman calls it. The limits to poise vary from person to person. For instance, some people blush more readily than others do.

The prisoner and the flower

An individual may give other hints of his basic temperamental factors, such as regularity, distractibility or shyness, that seem to be in part genetically determined. He also emits signals of his bodily characteristics, including his stature, sex and skin colour. And because everyone has the dangerous tendency to classify and type other people instantly, these characteristics affect the ways in which other people treat him. By mirroring and amplifying his peculiarities they force him to conform to the impression he creates, or to camouflage his characteristics. It is along lines such as these that the biological and the sociological view of individuality will have to be reconciled. There are real brains, real bodies and real life-histories, so the concept of the distinct individual, blurred though he may be in Erving Goffman's analysis, cannot be empty.

'There is no one-to-one correspondence between human beings and persons.' So says an Oxford philosopher of science, Rom Harré. He is one of those who, in the 1970s, are attempting new approaches to personality from a social standpoint. He finds inspiration in Goffman's method of analysing adult behaviour in terms of roles, rules and rituals. In Iona and Peter Opie's records of children's play Harré sees the youngsters, too, finding out how to do things in the socially approved manner. He is fascinated by nicknames, in his own observations of children, and suspects that each age-grade may have traditional offices, designated Fatty, Piggy, Fleabag, Tombstone, and so forth. Each of these offices has a characteristic 'front' (Tombstone, for example, is a special clown) and is filled by a child able and willing to play the role.

The traditional rival schools of psychology have erred in not taking seriously the enormous social competence of ordinary people and their skilful theorising about one another. The essence of the human conspiracy, in Harré's opinion, is that everyone is to be regarded as a valuable and rational being, and each person is wholly dependent on his ability to get other people to understand him and support him. When one comes to personality, each person should be considered a unique universe, requiring a unique science to discover its elements, history and processes. He is no longer an object for study, like an atom or a monkey, but a participant who can give valuable, though not perfect, accounts of his behaviour. And although a person may work reliably, or speak truculently, in particular circumstances, his personality should not be dredged for fixed qualities, like reliability or truculence, because these are illusory abstractions. Instead, one should look to his resources for social competence.

A person is 'a process in time' and biography is all-important. Famous public figures like Napoleon and Abraham Lincoln have had many biographers, yet each new account by a competent historian, even today, sheds new light on their experiences, motives and behaviour. To imagine trying to assess such individuals by a standard personality questionnaire ('Are you interested in dances and parties?') would seem self-evidently an impertinence. Yet a private person leading an unremarkable life is not significantly less complex or mysterious than the famous, and many psychologists profess to evaluate his personality by such 'instant' means.

If the assumption is that each person is a universe, even a partial assessment of his personality will be extremely time-consuming. At first thought, it might seem impossible ever to pursue research along these lines, except with some opulent Narcissus who could afford a retinue of psychiatrists and psychologists. Where, otherwise, could you find a person in good physical health, and the resources to pay for a thorough investigation of his personality? The answer, it turns out, is in the Belgian prison service.

Jean-Pierre De Waele, dean of psychology at the Free University of Brussels, is also the prison service's chief psychiatrist. In that capacity he has to provide information when a question arises whether a prisoner serving a life sentence might be released. The Minister of Justice may think that particularly careful investigation is necessary in the case of a person who has already committed more than one murder, before he decides whether to let the prisoner go. These are special circumstances: prisoners who have all the time in the world and authorities who are anxious to make wise decisions. De Waele has therefore been able to institute assessments of individual personalities which seem to be without precedent in their thoroughness. A team of psychiatrists, psychologists and social workers deals with a small number of individuals, each of whom can be studied for as much as a full year. The prisoners give their cooperation because they know that a favourable report would be their best chance of freedom.

A prisoner undergoing a 'systematic personality assessment' will spend some months writing his autobiography, and he explains his account in many sessions. But the investigators also make their own enquiries in the places where the prisoner has lived, and with people who knew him. With this independent source of biographical information, they can look for significant omissions or errors in the prisoner's account, at the same time as they are building up their own inventory of his former circumstances and behaviour. Meanwhile, others in De Waele's team observe his activities and behaviour in the various settings of ordinary prison life. And, for further insight, they set him special problems and see how he tackles them.

A problem may be deliberately contrived to create a certain amount of stress. For example, the prisoner is asked to remain within a marked space and recover a flower from a vase that is beyond arm's reach. He is given equipment such as pieces of wood and a chair, which are helpful, and other paraphernalia which are not, and he is told there are three solutions. In fact there are only two (one using the wood and the other the chair) and after he has found those two, the psychiatric team will keep him trying for the legendary third solution, with the promise of continuing the next day if need be.

The watchers record the prisoner's behaviour carefully, as he shifts from being puzzled to being bored, despairing, exasperated or angry. He may become suspicious of the test – that is one of the known possible reactions – but he has to continue with it, until the team has formed a thorough impression of his behaviour under stress. What matters is not the display of some explosive end result or of an alleged behavioural 'trait', but the processes of action and expression which unfold during successive episodes in the prisoner's attempts to solve the problem.

Shapes, masks and motives

Drawbacks to this way of pursuing research into personality are plain enough. The reports on each prisoner so investigated are voluminous and difficult either for Jean-Pierre De Waele and his associates to publish or for their professional colleagues to digest. The conclusions that bear upon the practical issue of the prisoner's release are confidential. Only a very small number of individuals can be studied in this fashion and, as they are prisoners convicted of serious crimes, they may be in some respects unrepresentative of individual human nature as it exists in the general population. And then, of course, some social scientists question the involvement of psychiatry with law-enforcement and also the use of deceptive psychological tests. Against all that must be set De Waele's conviction that only by thorough assessments, of the kind made possible by the unusual circumstances, can one escape from the glibness and sterility of previous attempts to describe individuals in a scientific fashion.

De Waele in Brussels and Rom Harré in Oxford are together elaborating an 'ethogenic' theory of personality assessment. In evolutionary terms they think that apes have personalities, too. But the organisation of the social competences that constitute personality became much more highly developed during the origin of human beings – and also much more flexible, as instinct receded in human behaviour. Child development and body shape give De Waele and Harré other perspectives. Two important metamorphoses occur, the first coming at about six years, when bodily proportions change from those of an 'infant' to those of a 'child' and, significantly, the individual begins to participate in the social rituals and performances of the children's culture.

The second metamorphosis, at puberty, is often marked by physical awkwardness, but thereafter the individual has assumed the physical proportions and 'body type' that he will possess, in a fairly stable form, through his adult life. De Waele and Harré see important physiological and psychological consequences of body type. Other people expect certain kinds of behaviour from an individual according to his appearance and the individual tends to satisfy these expectations.

'Let me have men about me that are fat,' Julius Caesar remarked, according to Shakespeare. 'Yon Cassius has a lean and hungry look . . . ' To digress a little from the main thesis of De Waele and Harré, investigators in the past have principally distinguished three tendencies in body types, and their extreme characteristics, as follows:

round and fat ('pyknic' or 'endomorph'): relaxed, sociable and extraverted

long and thin ('leptosome' or 'ectomorph'): inhibited, secretive and introverted

broad and strong ('athletic' or 'mesomorph'): agressive and adventurous

There are also correlations with bodily disease, the round and fat being more vulnerable to diabetes than the others, the long and thin to tuberculosis, and the broad and strong to coronaries. In one modern interpretation, the round and fat body form resembles that of the infant-child metamorphosis, while the long and thin resembles the body form of puberty.

De Waele and Harré clearly separate personality from the 'personas' or 'fronts' that an individual presents to other people. As far as personas are concerned, commonsense legitimately rules, because each culture has a repertoire of 'types' which a person can act, and which other people recognise him to be acting; each person can have more than one persona. The social competences represented in personality, on the other hand, flow from the cognitive and symbolic processes of human 'self-domestication'. Motives, in this theory, are not mysterious 'drives' but are merely part of the account that a human being gives to explain his actions and plans; intentions and wants are of the same kind. People know a lot more about the causes and reasons for their conduct than presumptuous psychologists commonly suppose.

Thus De Waele and Harré take a large step forward in demystifying personality, and a large step back from the hope of quick assessments and diagnoses. Their ideas are a powerful antidote to any arrogant scientific notion that people are simple to understand. But the sheer impracticability of producing a thousand pages of close analysis on more than a few unusual individuals may well doom De Waele's and Harré's assessment methods to the sidelines of psychology.

South-Sea cricket

In the Trobriand Islands of Papua New Guinea, people know rather precisely who they are. In these islands, sixty years ago, Bronislaw Malinowski studied the life and culture of the people so effectively that he created the modern style of anthropological research. He feared that missionaries and traders would destroy the old way of life, but in the 1970s Trobriand culture is still vigorous. They have an airstrip and a bus service on the main island, and many children go to school. There are useful implements of iron and steel. But the economic and social systems are neolithic and axe-like pieces of stone serve as special money. When I sat eating yams in a Trobriand village, watching the bare-

Cricketers, Trobriand style (top right). *They come on to the field dressed as if for war and this team is pretending to be an aircraft that is coming in to land. Giving and taking, Trobriand style* (below). *A person has died and everyone who knew him becomes involved in elaborate exchanges that confirm their relationships.*

breasted girls go by, or observing the butchery of a pig with a fire-hardened stick driven into the heart, I did not have to imagine myself back in the Stone Age – I was there. And the principal impression was not of dirt but of dignity.

Any individual, anywhere in the world, finds his social and personal identity in his network of social relationships, which generally refer to the membership of a number of different groups. No two people can stand in exactly the same relationship to the same combination of groups, so individuality can be defined in this social way, as well as by genetic, bodily or mental differences. And defining oneself is an important and continuing issue for each person. In this respect, these stone-age villagers, living in their traditional culture, are more secure than many people in industrialised countries, where social groupings are often shortlived.

A Trobriand islander is a reincarnated spirit and a member of his mother's clan. He lives in his mother's brother's village, as an heir to his uncle's wealth, if any; also to his uncle's secret magic, whether it is for making yams grow or rain fall, or for navigating the reef-ridden sea. A man in his turn is responsible for supplying his sisters with food from his yam garden, and for adopting their children. His father, who brought him up as a child, belongs to a different clan and lives in another village. That is only the start of his repertoire of group loyalties – of his affiliations and responsibilities within his clan, his family and in-laws, among his fellow villagers, and with friends in other parts of the island. Each link in the network is confirmed by elaborate giving and receiving of food.

When somebody dies, the islanders systematically trace out their networks of groups and relationships. Hundreds of dollars' worth of goods (a great deal of wealth by Trobriand standards) change hands after a death, according to very complicated rules. They reorganise relationships between people who were formerly linked by the dead man. Such giving and taking reconfirms the bonds of altruism that death might otherwise break. It is all done publicly to prevent cheating, and the exchanges glue Trobriand society together.

In the 1970s, the problem for the Trobrianders is how to join the world and the twentieth century on their own terms, preserving continuity with their traditions. It is an extreme version of the problem facing people everywhere, as the human world changes its technologies and ways of life faster than ever before. Papua New Guinea, of which the Trobriands are a part, has won independence and thus a place in international politics. More and more islanders are travelling to the mainland for Western-style studies. Some of them have read Malinowski. A trickle of tourists has threatened to become a flood, their cameras gulping up pictures of semi-nudity and quaint ways. But if Malinowski were still alive, his fears for the vulnerability of Trobriand culture might be allayed by watching them play cricket.

The old English game was introduced by a former administrator, but an Englishman would hardly recognise it as cricket now. The islanders have adapted the game to their own ways. For a start, it is played only after an exceptional yam harvest, and it symbolises the broader rivalry between the competing villages. There can be any number of men in each team, provided the opponents have the same number: in England eleven, in the Trobriands perhaps ninety. The teams come on to the field dressed as for war, but their war-dances are modern. One team comes on as an 'aircraft' which banks and circles the field and then 'lands'. Out of it comes a troop of soldiers armed with hand grenades – and a tourist.

Kula. Confections of shells of little intrinsic worth but having rich associations are exchanged, at great trouble and expense, by hazardous canoe voyages between the islands of the Western Pacific.

The game is played with home-made bats and balls. When a batsman is out, his opponents pronounce him *dead*. They perform a triumphal chant, according to the method of his disposal. For a catch it is the 'PK' chant, from PK chewing gum which makes your fingers sticky. A tally of leaves keeps the score, but ancient styles of Trobriand politics intrude. Quite regardless of the true score, the home team will win, preferably by a small margin.

The anthropology of ancient customs is of necessity giving way to an anthropology of change. And Trobriand islanders have an ongoing story to tell about their adaptation to the modern world, as they gamble their traditions and livelihood in a bold experiment. A young man called John Kasaipwalova went to Australia as a student. He came back with the most potent magic that anyone can remember and, at the age of twenty-four, he led a cultural revolution in the Trobriand Islands. In 1973, he was elected leader of the local council, and quite soon abolished the council, because it represented the outsiders, the government on the mainland.

Nowadays you may find John Kasaipwalova staging a play, driving a bus or talking politics. But in particular he is an entrepreneur, running a cooperative village development corporation. He knows the jargon of economists and bankers and he is working for material progress, but within the framework of his island's culture. The movement he leads is hoping to introduce rice-growing in otherwise useless swamp land. He has planned a tourist hotel on a good beach, but it will consist of a village of huts, Trobriand-style, and it will cater for only a few dozen visitors at a time. The wood-carvers of the island are being nurtured, and persuaded not to content themselves with pieces that sell easily, or with traditional work; they are to invent new devices that reflect the changing times. But the manner in which John Kasaipwalova wants to see his fellow-Trobrianders make contact with the modern world is best represented in the Kula, Malinowski's most celebrated discovery and the islanders' greatest pride.

The Trobrianders are descendants of great navigators of prehistory who peopled the islands of the wide ocean, taking their pigs and yams with them. And travels by canoe beyond the horizon are still required for the Kula. It involves scattered islands, forming a ring 700 miles in circumference. Clockwise around it, necklaces made of red shells travel from island to island, from hand to hand, in an endless chain. In repeated exchanges for the necklaces, white armshells circulate in the opposite direction. They are of no practical use, and no one is supposed to retain a piece for long.

Yet each Kula piece has its own history and to any islander who possesses it briefly it brings pride and honour. He has to make decisions about passing it on to a partner in another island, as a gift – but a gift that ought to be matched or surpassed by a reciprocal gift, another Kula piece, some time. The finely judged generosity and trust and misgivings make the Kula trade a working model of other elaborate, but often more confused systems of give-and-take. And by his efforts the successful Kula trader becomes an active member of a wider world beyond his own small coral island.

From the industrialised countries many anthropologists have gone to stare at exotic people, in the hope of glimpsing truths about mankind in the mirror of their primitiveness. Now, disconcertingly, we find the exotic people staring back at us, as when John Kasaipwalova explains the 'magic' that he brought back from his student days in Australia. Most white men, the *dimdims*, came to the Trobriand Islands not to learn, as Malinowski did, but to tell the people how to live. Their ways

117

were strange and baffling to unschooled minds. In the foreigner's world, a man who took much wealth for his private use was a great man; for the Trobrianders, a great man was one who gave much wealth away. The foreigners nevertheless had machinery that dazzled the islanders, who imagined a sublime civilisation lying behind the self-assurance of the visitors. But when John Kasaipwalova went to Australia he found, instead, class hatred, racial prejudice, the rat-race, crime, smoke, and lonely young people in big cities doubting the values of their civilisation. These were the foreigners who would tell the Trobrianders how to live. Such was the simple knowledge that made John Kasaipwalova determined to work for his own people's way of life. He wants not to preserve it like a museum piece but to see it evolving to meet the modern world, keeping the Kula-trader's sense of equal partnership in the human adventure.

Few of the brown-skinned people of the Pacific have been so fortunate in their isolation.

The coloured dolls

As Erving Goffman observes: 'To be awkward or unkempt, to move or talk wrongly, is to be a dangerous giant, a destroyer of worlds.' A person deemed to be abnormal, perhaps because he stammers, creates embarrassment. Other people may pretend not to notice the abnormality, but the person carrying the stigma may notice that they are pretending not to notice. Anyone whose skin colour does not conform to the majority is also liable to be stigmatised. Dwarves, cripples, disfigured people, the mentally ill, homosexuals and women in a men's world may all in effect be marked for life in the same kind of way. The stigmatised person may be torn between loyalty to himself and his minority group and a reluctant desire to conform to social norms that decree what the typical behaviour of a member of the stigmatised minority should be.

An American black, for instance, may find himself clowning the part of a 'typical' black in the presence of whites, rather than risk provoking conflict: the impersonation of blacks by blacks has been called 'minstrelisation'. But the member of a black minority who, on the contrary, tries to prove that he is a cultivated gentleman by the standards of the white majority, despite the general reputation of his kind, may stand accused of another kind of treachery. There may be no way out of this quandary except militancy on behalf of one's own kind, which typically involves a political stance and a mirroring of white contempt for black by black contempt for white. Whatever way he turns, it is impossible for a member of a stigmatised minority to lead a 'normal' life.

White New Zealanders, living in the land of the Maoris that was colonised by the British, have prided themselves on peaceful race relations, but there were always latent tensions. Now, with Maoris moving into the towns in greater numbers and with Polynesian islanders also settling in New Zealand, the tensions come to the surface more often. For fifteen years Graham Vaughan, a psychologist at Auckland University, has been studying the development of racial attitudes in New Zealand children, white and Maori. The technique he uses was originally developed in the United States some thirty years ago, where it showed a curious inversion, in which black children identified themselves with whites.

You can ask a six-year-old white child which of two dolls, pink or brown, he would choose to give a little girl. He will favour the pink doll. You can show him pairs of pictures of whites and Maoris and ask which one is more lazy, for instance, and he may point out a Maori; ask him which is more clever and he may

Identity tests. With 'white' and 'Maori' drawings researchers in New Zealand explore the racial attitudes of children.

indicate a white; ask him which he would prefer as a playmate and again he may select a white youngster. The white child seems to have assimilated the prejudices of his community: in fact, by the age of six, whites are at the peak of their racial prejudice in favour of whites. But then repeat the tests with a Maori child of the same age. He may choose the pink doll and declare that the Maori in the picture is lazy, the white is clever and he would like to play with a white child. There are variations – perhaps with the Maori child judging the Maoris to be cleaner, say – that show that the judgements are not mechanical. At the age of six Maori children quite strongly identify with white people rather than with Maoris.

In an unequal situation, the young Maori likes what he sees on the other side of the racial fence. So much does he want to be a part of it that he imagines himself as one of 'them'. It is an attitude that cuts deep, while the child searches for his social identity. But circumstances are changing in New Zealand. There is a Brown Power movement nowadays. And the traumatic period when young Maoris come to accept that they *are* Maoris and members of the underprivileged group begins earlier in cities like Auckland than it used to do, or still does in rural areas. It starts at eight years of age instead of twelve.

Anyone who is disturbed by the results in younger Maori children is conniving with the children, in taking their indications of their colour preferences to be socially important. No one can suppose that a child does not know what colour his own skin is; the paradoxical identification with whites is as much wilful as wishful. But in deeming it to be noteworthy the onlooker may be thinking: 'How sad, that this child does not face up to the fact that he has a dark face!' The onlooker is then being more than literal-minded. He is accepting a 'fact of life' that others are trying to turn into a non-fact – that the colour of a person's skin is significant in the societies in which we live. He is trying to enforce a stigma.

Nevertheless, the findings about self-identifications among children are not just shedding a sidelight on race relations. Their implications are altogether broader. They show the beginnings, in childhood, of group alignments in a hostile situation. From only four years old, in fact, a child is ready and eager to play the game of group identity and intergroup rivalry.

A choice of rewards

Here are two tests in which the reader can take part. They may say something about your human nature. Look carefully at this random mass of dots and you will see a number two among them.

The same idea is at work in the following pair of patterns but you will see a number more easily in one than in the other. Decide which one it is, where the number is plainest.

Julius

Augustus

The left-hand number shows more clearly for so-called Julius persons, while if a number jumps out first from the right-hand pattern, you are an Augustus person. Decide whether you are a Julius or an Augustus. Be honest about it, and remember which group you belong to. The meaning of this test will become clear later.

The second test concerns a different kind of decision. It has to do with allocating rewards when there is not much information. Suppose you have to advise a wealthy man on how to divide gifts of money totalling £15 between two other people who are not present. In fact, you do not know precisely who the recipients are; all you know is that one of them is one of the Julius group, and the other is one of the Augustus people. There is no benefit at all to yourself. The money can be split in any of the following ways:

To the member of the

Julius group	3	5	7	8	10	12
To the member of the	or	or	or	or	or	
Augustus group	12	10	8	7	5	3

To be quite clear about the options, the first one means that £3 goes to the member of the Julius group and £12 to the member of the Augustus group. Please arrive at your decision before reading any further. In fact, make a careful mental note of exactly what reward you give to the Julius person and what to the Augustus person.

The latter test is based on experiments carried out a few years ago at the University of Bristol by Henri Tajfel and his collaborators. On the basis of their results in this kind of decision-making, I shall venture to guess what your own decision was, about the rewards. You probably gave either £8 or £10 to Julius and either £7 or £5 to Augustus. Possibly you went the whole way and gave £12 to Julius and £3 to Augustus, but it is unlikely that you actually gave less to Julius than to Augustus.

Behind my guess is firstly the supposition that you have decided that you are a Julius person. The pattern of dots labelled 'Augustus' on the previous page is a nonsense; there is no number there and I must beg forgiveness for the deception. Secondly, the experiments in Bristol have shown that it is only necessary to tell a person that he is a member of a group for him to act in a way favourable to that group. That is to say, most people, in a test such as this, allocate more money to members of their own group than to members of the other group. It happens even though they do not know who the members of the different groups are, or what their characteristics are, never mind who the individual recipients may be. Finally, if that is the norm of 'groupness', there is another norm of 'fairness', and people generally strike a balance between the two: hence my suggestion that you chose one of the lesser options favouring the Julius group, rather than the extreme. Provided, of course, that I guessed right, you may by now have sensed how startling this kind of result is.

The original experiments involved boys of fourteen and fifteen, who came in parties from their school. Each party consisted of boys who knew one another well. Various pretences were used to divide the boys into groups: they were asked to guess the numbers of dots in a succession of clusters, or else to say which they preferred out of a succession of pairs of paintings by Paul Klee and Wassily Kandinsky. But the tests were doubly deceptive because the experimenters disregarded the results and assigned each boy at random to the 'underestimator' and 'overestimator' groups, or to the 'Klee group' and 'Kandinsky group'. A boy did not know who the other members of his group were. But he was given tables (with more choices than I provided) to assign, rewards for example, to 'Number 15 of the Klee group' and 'Number 21 of the Kandinsky group'. Actual money was at stake; each point was worth about 0·04p and each boy eventually went home with about 40p. The main results, showing a pronounced bias in favour of one's own ingroup, were as I have already described. But boys who were asked to assign rewards to two people in one group, either the ingroup or the outgroup, went for maximum fairness.

Some of the tests introduced variations in the total amount to be allocated. This allowed the experimenters to create situations in which the boys might, for instance, try to get as much money as possible for their colleagues out of the experimenters ('maximum joint profit'). Or they had the opportunity to go for the highest possible reward for the member of their ingroup, regardless of what the member of the outgroup was getting ('maximum ingroup profit'). But it turned out that neither of these possibilities was as attractive as the choices which gave the largest *difference* in reward between the ingroup and outgroup members ('maximum difference').

In short, the boys were willing to forgo maximum profits in order to sustain a substantial difference between their own group and the outgroup; they were prepared to pay, in effect, for the privilege of being 'one up' on the outgroup. In most instances, the norm of 'fairness' continued to exercise a moderating effect on the various policies favouring the ingroup. But when variable totals were to be distributed between two boys of the same group a difference appeared: the assigners went for maximum joint profit more assiduously on behalf of two ingroup members than for two outgroup members. This represented, in Tajfel's words, 'a clear case of gratuitous discrimination.'

Shifting norms

As an ebullient leader among social psychologists in Europe, Henri Tajfel is a friendly but stern critic of the American tradition in his subject. One of his complaints is about the neglect of the crucial social problems of conflict, prejudice, discrimination and hostility between groups. The reason, as he sees it, comes from too great an emphasis on dealings between individuals, as if war and peace, for instance, were just the psychology of the individual writ large. This approach neglects the *social* psychology of intergroup behaviour, which involves actions of individuals in unison. The unison arises because people live in a social context that has its own laws and structure.

The antecedents of the research into 'groupness' at the University of Bristol are worth noting. More than twenty years ago, at a boy's camp, Muzafer Sherif and Carolyn Sherif of the University of Oklahoma carried out a memorable experiment in group conflict. The camp opened with three days of miscellaneous activities for the boys, who were about twelve years old. Then they were divided into two groups, the Red Devils and Bull Dogs; the Sherifs deliberately put boys who had been friendly with each other into different groups. Fostering ingroup loyalty and hostility towards the outgroup, with competitive games, proved to be all too easy. After an engineered incident involving damaged cakes, the two groups fought earnest battles with table knives, dishes and apples, and raided each other's huts. The Sherifs hurriedly terminated the experiment.

This 'war' in miniature was a product of deliberate indoctrination and of real issues between the two groups of boys. But in thinking about the character of group hostility, Tajfel amd his colleagues suspected that there might be a 'generic norm' of discrimination against any outgroups, which did not necessarily depend upon pre-existing prejudice or conflicts of interest. They therefore planned a series of experiments to find out just how much a person needed to know about groups

and allegiances before he began to identify himself with one group as opposed to another. The tests described in the previous pages were meant to be simply control experiments. No discrimination was really expected when the person knew nothing except that he had been assigned to an unexplained group for a flimsy reason. But even in these unpropitious conditions, the 'generic norm' showed up at once, and unmistakably.

In a strictly materialist sense, 'groupness' can be irrational, for example when a boy forgoes the maximum reward for a fellow group-member in order to maximise the difference between the rewards to the ingroup and the outgroup. Tests in children, like those among the Maoris and whites in New Zealand, show that strong identification with a group can start very early in life. Biologists will certainly wonder whether such promptness among people, in identifying with a group, represents another biological bias in human behaviour. Is Tajfel's 'generic norm' of discrimination in favour of ingroups also a 'genetic norm'?

The evolutionists whom we met in Chapter I have something to say about the contrast between the comradeship within human groups and the hostility between groups. 'The inward harmony and the outward snarl' is how William Hamilton refers to it. He thinks the very support that reciprocal altruism, give-and-take, affords to the growth and diversification of social systems tends to undermine the basis of its own success. It depends on an ability to remember who has been helpful and who has cheated. We are all potential cheaters, so the argument goes, but the outsider who will never show his face again has more chance of getting away with it. Evolution may therefore have favoured diligence and speed in human powers in distinguishing who can and who cannot be trusted. Group membership is a guide: any kind of group of which one is a member is a potential arena for give-

and-take, while groups of which one is not a member are potential sources of enemies or cheats. From this point of view, then, the Bristol experiments might be tapping a motivation, sanctioned by natural selection, to discriminate between 'us' and 'them'.

But which really comes first, a threat from hostile outsiders, or the building of an ingroup? To Tajfel, that is a further crucial question that has been neglected, amid the emphasis on individual psychology and on the roots of hostility. Obviously, dangers from outside can assist or intensify the building of an ingroup. But the way humans value the distinctiveness and comradeship of their own groups, in their quest for social identity, must be regarded as something much more positive than hostility.

To be discriminating in your choice of colleagues and friends, and then to show them special attention and favours, does not necessarily imply hostility to anyone else, any more than choosing a husband or wife means that you hate all other members of the opposite sex. Nor any more than forming a swimming club is a sign of hostility to non-swimmers. All this is trite as soon as it is stated, but it has been curiously by-passed by those who have tried to understand the pathologies of intergroup behaviour in terms of innate wickedness or political tensions. If the virtue and value of ingroup behaviour are not taken into account, you are, as it were, trying to understand disease in an organ without knowing what the organ does when it is healthy.

The experiments that began with the Bristol schoolboys have given points of reference in a broad ocean of human social behaviour that previously seemed unnavigable for science. Many a theory had been launched in vain. Some, like those of Sigmund Freud and Konrad Lorenz, offered the innate aggressiveness of the individual as the source of conflict between groups – a world war being somehow like a pub brawl

Non-verbal communication. It is often easy to tell who is with whom, and when somebody is adopting 'role distance' to make a joke.

that got out of hand. Freud presumed a regression to infantile behaviour when individuals formed into groups. Other theories have emphasised the crowds that can seem imbued with passion, devoid of reason, and acting pathologically like stampeding cattle. But all that is beside the point.

The problem all along has been to explain why kindly and sane young men can be so easily persuaded to go out, not in a frenzied horde but in dignified formation, to stick bayonets into other young men or to drop napalm on women and children. A real and drastic shift occurs in the norms of human behaviour, as one goes from the conduct of the individual towards other individuals, to the conduct of an individual as a member of a group distinguished from other groups. Of course, during encounters between individuals people are also conscious of group identities, while aspects of an individual's behaviour in ingroup situations may persist during outgroup confrontations, perhaps to moderate his actions. But only by grasping the full import of the positive and quick propensity of human beings to identify with any group they find themselves in can one make a firm base from which to search out the origins of hostility. That Tajfel and his colleagues, at Bristol and elsewhere in Europe, have proceeded to do, developing the idea of the 'generic norm' of group behaviour to deal with relations between 'superior' and 'inferior' groups.

Experimental rebellion

Parents should perhaps be chary of sending their sons away to summer camps, in case they meet a tricky social psychologist. It was in another camp for boys that French experimenters arranged for a competition between two groups to see which could build a better hut. One group of boys was deliberately given poorer materials with which to work. Their response was interesting: they created a fenced garden around the hut and then argued that, taking the hut and garden together, their effort was better. In other words, with inferiority staring them in the face, in the matter of huts, they sought to alter the basis for comparison between the groups.

More recently, a study in the Netherlands has compared attitudes of engineering students at different colleges generally reckoned to be 'superior' or 'inferior' in their academic standing. Those at the 'inferior' college, when asked about the qualities needed in an engineer, emphasised practical abilities, in which they felt they compared more favourably with the other students. Building on such findings, it becomes possible to explore systematically the ways in which group behaviour depends upon people's perception of the situation prevailing between the groups, and to see how hostility and conflict arise from the prevailing beliefs in a society.

People may, for instance, feel secure and satisfied in their social identity and status. They may, on the other hand, feel insecure about the prospects of maintaining a position of superiority, or perhaps be dissatisfied with a position of completely unjust inferiority. John Turner has conducted experiments at Bristol in which groups of university arts students and groups of science students are asked to carry out tasks and to compare their efforts with those of another group. For example, a group of arts students may be asked to prepare a report on whether suicide is justifiable. The experimenter may tell them, quite casually, that arts students are better than science students at this kind of task. He thus sows the idea that arts students are members of the superior group. The experimenter may go on to remark, though, that their apparent superiority may be due to bias on somebody's part against scientific ways of thinking. That suggests to the arts students that their superiority may not be legitimate. The experimenter may then add that the findings about whether the arts students are better or not are inconsistent. So a third idea is sown: the situation is unstable because of the 'inconsistent' findings.

The consequence of giving such a gentle succession of hints is striking and predictable, from Turner's experiments. Confronted with the report of a science group, this arts group will mark it very severely. There is marked discrimination against an inferior group when the superior group feels insecure. It is a laboratory analogue of many real-life situations, for example the intensified repression of blacks in South Africa where a ruling white minority feels threatened.

In another experiment, a group of science students may also be told that arts students do better at the task, but that it's not surprising in view of the aptitudes and training of arts students, and anyway the findings are always the same. In other words, they are told that they are of inferior status, but that this situation is 'legitimate' or just, and also stable. If the students believe that the other group is really better than they are, how will they react to a report on suicide by arts students? They are likely to rate it better than their own. Such behaviour has very little to do with the individual talents and temperaments of the members of the group. A group is more kindly disposed towards another, regardless of whether it is inferior or superior, provided the distinction seems just and unalterable. This is the experimental equivalent of a peaceful feudal society.

> *The rich man in his castle,*
> *The poor man at his gate,*
> *God made them, high or lowly,*
> *And order'd their estate.*

How then do you create a rebellion? Turner has been able to try out all sorts of combinations of high status or low status, justly or unjustly assigned, in a stable or unstable situation. When the inferior group sees that the situation is unjust and unstable, it senses that it can change things and the experiment warms up. When you are down but fighting you emphasise virtues in your group that other people have ignored. For example, a group of allegedly inferior science students may become highly critical of an arts group report, and assure one another about the special powers and virtues of science and scientists. They are then saying, in effect, that 'science is beautiful,' much as real-life groups in a similar fix have said 'Black is beautiful'.

Experiments of this kind, going on in half a dozen European laboratories, are beginning to give real insight into the conditions in which groups repress one another, or rebel; also into the forms that the repression or rebellion takes. Lurking in all this research is a general question. Does the individual see his best hope for improving his lot to be a matter of moving individually, by merit or luck, upwards through the social system? Or does he look to joint action with the group of which he is a member to make life better for the whole group? Social mobility or social change?

It is another of Tajfel's complaints against much contemporary social psychology that it reflects the Western and especially American ideal of individual improvement through social mobility in a free society, where the individual interacts with others on behalf of himself. Such social psychology may grievously neglect social change by group action, with people interacting in terms of their respective groups, which is probably typical of a great deal of human behaviour.

Dialect and discord

In dealings between two groups who speak with different characteristic dialects, for example employers

with standard accents and workers with the local vernacular, the two sides vary their styles of speech depending on the intergroup situation. If they are being conciliatory, they will speak more and more like each other, the boss for example becoming less formal in his speech. But in a situation of conflict, both sides heighten the peculiarities of their own ways of speech, and sound less alike.

Speech styles and their stigmas count for a great deal in one human's evaluations of another. In Montreal, Wallace Lambert asked people to listen to different voices reading the same passage, and to give their opinions about the speakers. Different languages (English and French) and different dialects (Parisian French, Canadian French and non-standard Canadian French) were used. What the judges did not know was that the same individual might be speaking twice, in different dialects; they then gave him quite different scores for matters like intelligence, dependability and height, simply according to the social rating of the dialect. And even judges who themselves spoke with a stigmatised dialect would downgrade people like themselves.

The dialect of Liverpool, made internationally familiar by the Beatles, is changing in subtle ways. 'Looch ous!' you may hear a playing child shout, meaning 'look out'. Some older Liverpudlians would say 'looch outs!', but the final replacement of 't' by 's' is an innovation. The same sort of story can be told from other cities: New York, Paris and London are among the places where ongoing shifts in dialect have been detected. Radio, television and education are widely supposed to be making people speak more and more alike. Rural dialects are indeed in retreat, but in the cities local forms of language continue to evolve very rapidly in our lifetimes.

The little changes in the way people talk set us on our last excursion into current research on human behaviour – in some ways the most fascinating. It relates closely to the behaviour of groups that we have been dealing with; also to the interactions between individuals considered earlier, because people adjust their speech to the occasion. This linguistic research is highly relevant, too, to comparisons of human performance, among individual children or between different cultures, touched on in previous chapters. There are even parallels to be found in the behaviour of animals. And the research bears equally upon this year's racial strife and on what was going on among human groups thousands of years ago. Fellow-experts will identify the work of the outstanding sociolinguist, William Labov, from this catalogue of clues.

Labov travels far and wide, with his tape-recorder, catching the nuances of everyday speech among ordinary people, which he can then analyse by computer. As well as having an unusual talent for engaging strangers in conversation, Labov disregards potential hostility and danger; he will set off briskly down the Falls Road in Belfast, for example, seemingly unaware that his associates are fearful for his safety. It is a necessary part of his work, because important changes in language are associated with tensions between human groups.

Some fifteen years have passed since Labov found that the dialect of the islanders of Martha's Vineyard off Massachusetts was reverting to a use of vowel sounds that people had when they first settled in the island in the seventeeth century. He identified the reason. New settlers had come, Portuguese immigrants, and consciously or unknowingly the local people were asserting their local identity. In the process they were excluding the strangers from their ingroup talk. Since then Labov has found comparable changes occurring in many other places in the United States and Europe.

Some of the clearest changes are to be found in his home city of Philadelphia, where he works at the University of Pennsylvania (Erving Goffman is a colleague). Philadelphians' manners of speech reflect a tense and hostile situation. In the residential neighbourhoods, blacks and whites live side by side, but the lines between them are drawn very sharply, and the dialects on the two sides are becoming more and more different. Not only are vowel sounds changing but peculiar turns of phrase distinguish the inhabitants of the one city. For example, one person may say 'Service is bad anymore'; another may say 'I been know that'. The first speaker is necessarily a white, the second a black, and neither would use the other's expression. Such language breaks are less pronounced in England. But there, too, in cities where recent immigrants have settled, Liverpool included, Labov finds linguistic hints of the same kind of struggle for local identity. For him, the competition for jobs and local privileges is the kind of social force that lies behind language change.

Labov tells a story of the Cobras, a group of adolescents whom he knew in Harlem in New York. He noticed them always saying 'Let's tip', instead of 'Let's go'. One day Labov ventured to use the expression himself. Immediately the Cobras all pretended not to understand what he meant; he had presumed too far in trying to wear a mask of local identity.

But the real-life language in which he deals stands in refreshing contrast with the suppositions of grammarians, teachers and even the people who do the speaking. With his recordings Labov has demolished a popular idea of American educationists in the 1960s, that linguistic deprivation and associated mental incapacities prevailed among the young blacks of the ghettos. He describes the ghetto children bathed in verbal stimulation from morning to night and participating in competitive displays of verbal skill. He tells how children who seem tongue-tied in a formal situation become garrulous and clever in friendly arguments. And the 'nonstandard Negro English' that they speak is just as grammatical, by its own rules, as any prestigious dialect.

A manner of speaking

People are often unaware of the shifts in their language, even of innovations that they use themselves. William Labov asked a group of students what they thought was the commonest word or phrase used for leave-taking in present-day English. In other words, how do people say 'goodbye' nowadays? Only eight per cent of the votes were for 'byebye', but Labov's records show that to be by far the commonest form. With small variations, 'byebye' and 'bye' account for eighty-eight per cent of all leavetakings noted by Labov in America and England. Expressions like 'so long', 'see you' and 'goodnight' are scarcely used at all. Many people who say 'byebye' deny that they do so. 'Goodbye' has become too formal, just as 'God be with you' did before it. More intimacy, making the ritual of leave-taking appear less like a ritual, that seems to be what people are expressing. 'If speakers knew that they said "byebye",' Labov comments, 'they would immediately begin to say something else.'

The quest for greater intimacy is thus another reason for changes in a language, along with the wish to display membership of a local group. Labov discerns a third reason: the wish to be more vehement. And here strange reversals of meaning occur. The expression 'Service is bad anymore' was mentioned earlier as white Philadelphian talk. It means (in case you didn't work it out) 'Service is bad nowadays', the very opposite of 'service is bad, not anymore' which is the nearest familiar phrase. There is an implied double negative used for emphasis. The more blatant double negative 'Nobody knows nothing' has exactly the same meaning as 'nobody knows anything' but again with more vehemence – and never mind no pedants who might try to say otherwise. Many languages use double negatives or similar illogical devices for deliberate emphasis.

All of this bears upon the most fundamental question of linguistics: why do human beings not all speak the same language? If they did so, the human tongue would be a far better means of communication. Only an expert could tell that present-day languages from Ireland to Bangladesh stem from a common Indo-European root. Possibly the first modern humans, 40,000–50,000 years ago, used the common ancestor of every language on Earth. Geographical dispersal is one obvious reason for the differences, and there is good correspondence between genetic shifts among human populations and differences in language. If you can't breed together, you can't talk either. But separation did not make people run differently. It could produce linguistic change only if there was a continual tendency for languages to vary in any case. In fact this tendency is very vigorous; even an isolated village will show differences in real language between the generations, the sexes and the social classes.

Many changes involve the speaker in greater effort, in lengthening vowel sounds, for instance, or using extra words, as when someone says 'I'm going to walk' instead of 'I shall walk'. So the traditional idea that non-standard speech is typically lazy is false, even though clipped and slurred speaking often occurs. For Labov the reasons for language change are more positive, and of the kinds already mentioned. The codified, formal language of polite society erases the marks of local identity. It becomes weak, distant in its effect, clogged and confused. So the language has to change, usually from the vernacular 'below', to restore communication and break down barriers between human beings. The changes are themselves signals, quite apart from the literal meanings of particular remarks; they carry messages of intimacy, vehemence and group identity.

That is the essence of what Labov has to tell us. And then the animal behaviourist chimes in, to report that among the white-crowned sparrows of North America abrupt changes in dialect in the birds' song occur between adjacent populations. The young birds learn their own dialect between the ages of ten days and fifty days. The effect of the differences is to prevent interbreeding between the various populations, so it is a mechanism among the birds for the controlled closure of groups. It results in a certain amount of in-breeding, which implies a genetic basis for altruism and cooperation. There is a clear enough analogy with the sharp boundaries between human dialects of blacks and whites in the city of Philadelphia, but what the analogy means is debatable.

It is easy to see the ongoing dialect-formation among humans as something wholly sinister. Indeed, as I have shown, the whole business of group behaviour might be interpreted with pessimism. You could assert that we all have biological biases creating automatic hostility to other groups and encouraging us to confirm our hostility by speaking differently; William Hamilton outlines the evolutionary mechanisms to produce just such behaviour (see page 124). But it is also possible to place the emphasis, as Henri Tajfel and William Labov do, on more positive features. Language changes, in the first instance, bring people within a group closer together and enable them to communicate more vigorously.

Although there is plainly still a great deal to be found out about the facts of human group behaviour, and about its origins and implications, that is no excuse for not trying to make sense of the recent findings. They

suggest that human beings are in a difficult fix. To paraphrase Samuel Johnson: 'He who loves everybody loves nobody.' The more friendly people strive to be, the more exclusive their activities automatically become. In addition there are special altruistic exchanges, private jokes, private languages. Showing friendship involves attending to one person rather than another. Mere protestations of concern and friendship from a passer-by or distant acquaintance are rightly dismissed as polite rituals, if they are not accompanied by real evidence of group participation.

As Tajfel points out, the positive aspects of social identity can acquire meaning only in comparisons with other groups. Social history has to illuminate the question of why skin colour is more often a basis for intergroup comparisons than, say, eye colour. But the tone of comparisons can vary: one can either cultivate and exercise the supposed virtues of one's own group or, in a more negative and derogatory fashion attack the other group.

The existence of exclusive groups sets the stage for mistrust, hostility and war, and the metaphor of the conspiracy becomes all too apt. What is to blame for this unsatisfactory state of affairs? Our genes? Our culture? Neither, unless you are to complain that they have not made us into hydra-like supermen capable of personally demonstrating to four billion other people that we love them dearly.

The human dilemma. Friendliness and cooperation within one group of people all too easily sets the stage for antagonism towards other groups. (Detail from 'The Tower of Babel').

Postscript

Image and agenda

At the start of this brisk journey through some current research in social behaviour I promised no over-arching theory, only a metaphor. Useful pieces of theory, such as those about the relationship of language to social context, and the alternative models for the evolution of altruism, help to strengthen links between different areas of study. But infants who reorganise their knowledge into higher and more complex systems may regress a little in what they know; so may the students of human behaviour. They may even be better off without big theories, because theory in human affairs is the mother of a certainty and grandmother of fanaticism. Remember, too, the suggestion from De Waele and Harré that each person is a universe itself, requiring its own theories.

The new styles of research described in this book show no sign of coming to an end for want of a big theory. For instance, knowledge of primates and of human cultures may need rehearsing to test the reality of various forms of altruism and spoiled altruism envisaged in the little evolutionary theories. The understanding of infancy is benefiting greatly from the study of interactions, both between biology and experience and between the child and other people. Similar studies ought to be extended to all ages, notably to puberty which so far has had much less attention than infancy. The resolution of nature versus nurture, item by item, has only just begun and many aspects of behaviour await further investigation. Crime, for instance, now seems to have very little heredity in its origins. And a fascinating question is how the genetic determinants of an individual's temperament influence all his social attitudes.

Research on mother-child interactions and on recovery from malnutrition are instances of research topics that already have practical applications. Experimental anthropology has a direct bearing on policies for education and innovation, not only in the developing countries but in industrialised countries as well. A further example of applications of the new research styles comes from the apparent success of Michael Argyle's group at Oxford, in treating mental illness by teaching people how to behave more effectively in face-to-face interactions. The scope for extending the studies on group behaviour is almost unlimited, not just through contrived experiments but also in tracing the real-life analogues of the laboratory work, including the development of group loyalties in children. Research on groupness must eventually connect more clearly both with biological studies of the roots of group behaviour and with cultural studies of how membership of a tribe or nation affects the way people think. Game theory will continue to illuminate the compromises that people make between different norms of behaviour.

Even if we have to wait indefinitely for a big theory, people will still want to know what general image of the human being science has to offer. The individual conspirator that emerges from all of the foregoing is neither saint nor villain. In view of all the violence and injustice in the world, we cannot expect to fulfil Robert Burns' wish to 'prove the truth that Man is good by nature'. But we can get close. It seems that man by nature is disposed to be friendly. He is also disposed to learn and on the whole respect the norms of behaviour for his culture. Compared with other animals, human beings acquired many remarkable characteristics in their evolution, ranging from the precision finger-grip to the female orgasm. But recall three evolutionary trends of exceptional importance to social behaviour: (1) the growth of altruism between unrelated people; (2) the reduction in the murder rate; and (3) the almost total replacement of instinct by cultural learning from the group into which a baby is born.

Among the adult members of a group, recurrent tendencies to selfishness and cheating have to be kept continually in check by group action. Furthermore, friendliness within groups can actively feed hostility between groups. The most valuable service of evolution theory, social psychology and linguistics in recent years has been to make this supreme dilemma of 'us' versus 'them' clear for all to see. That may be the first step in learning to live with group behaviour.

Another issue is whether industrialised societies have not erred grievously in creating alien 'races' called children and adolescents, divorced in their interests from the adults. In more 'primitive' societies people grow up in adult company and the youngsters share increasingly in the excitements of public life, rather than having to engineer their own.

The ability to make predictions is a good test of a science. Ongoing research may show how to predict fairly precisely when loyalties will breed hostilities, when the underdog will find injustice intolerable, and when dominant groups will turn to repression. Reformers, revolutionaries and guardians of the *status quo* may all exploit this knowledge, but everyone may then be able to pursue their policies more wisely, more productively and perhaps less violently. Clearly there are also limits to the rate of change of cultures, beyond which individuals or communities will be liable to crack. In a world in which technological and political changes seem to proceed ever faster, the science of human behaviour may help to predict the point at which bold plans will be frustrated by human needs for continuity.

No one should suppose that science can ever provide absolution from politics or issues of morality. An explanation for wrongful behaviour is not a justification for it. The tensions between generosity and selfishness, and between group loyalties and wider responsibilities, are matters for vigilance and argument. Our nature commits us to being political animals, even when the constituency is no larger than a family. Fretting about issues of right and wrong is the price we have to pay for being more sentient than the ants, and for having the opportunity to make social progress. But a renewed sense of wonder about our privileged position in nature, and about the rich and vulnerable qualities of human life, may heighten political wisdom.

The growth of cities, nations and free connections between independent nations shows that the problems created by groupness can be solved, at least to an approximation. Constitutions and treaties serve better than force. Given some sense of justice, stability and mutual benefit, people who do not know one another can live close together in comparative harmony and peace. They still form a myriad of distinctive groups, because that is the nature and quality of human life. Moreover, an individual is a member of various groups and the conflicts and contrasts of loyalty that result may have a moderating effect on intergroup hostility. The overlapping identities of the individual are not as rich and well defined in Western society as they are in the Trobriand Islands, for example. The opportunities for fanaticism may therefore be greater in modern societies – a fanatic being typically a person who is preoccupied with a single ingroup-outgroup division.

The human community that embraces the whole planet has scarcely attempted yet to apply the principles of justice, mutual benefit and overlapping identities to the promotion of peace. One day, with effort and luck, all the earthlings will be courteous and considerate towards one another. But do not call it brotherly love. That was precisely what our ancestors moved beyond, a long time ago, when they entered the broader conspiracy of non-relatives.

Further Reading

There are more publications on human evolution, infant development and social behaviour than anyone could aspire to read. Much of the information in this book comes from recently published research papers and no other books cover just the same range of subject-matter. But the following books are recommended as thorough treatments of some of the most interesting areas of research dealt with briefly here. They are listed in order of relevance to the text.

Sociobiology: The New Synthesis by Edward O. Wilson (Belknap Press of Harvard University Press; Cambridge, Mass., 1975). A massive and masterly work that puts the evolution of human society into its zoological and theoretical context.

The Emergence of Man by John E. Pfeiffer (Harper & Row; New York, 1969 and Nelson; London, 1970). Valuable for its crosslinks between human evolution, primate studies and infant psychology.

The Interpretation of Cultures by Clifford Geertz (Basic Books; New York, 1973). A synthesis of ideas in cultural anthropology by an authority who emphasises the quest for meaning in myths and rituals.

Child Alive edited by Roger Lewin (Temple Smith; London, 1975). A collection of articles by some of the liveliest researchers on infancy.

The Integration of a Child into a Social World edited by Martin P. M. Richards (Cambridge University Press; London and New York, 1974). Another collection of articles on infancy, with more emphasis on social development and ideological factors.

Development in Infancy by T. G. R. Bower (W. H. Freeman; San Francisco and Reading, 1974). A controversial but penetrating analysis of the infant's growing understanding of the world.

Language and Social Man by M. A. K. Halliday (Longman; London, 1974). A concise account of language which emphasises the importance of meaning and the social context.

The Cultural Context of Learning and Thinking by Michael Cole, John Gay, Joseph A. Glick and Donald W. Sharp (Basic Books; New York, 1971 and Tavistock Publications; London, 1974). One of several accounts of the pioneering 'experimental anthropology' carried out in Liberia.

Children's Games in Street and Playground by Iona and Peter Opie (Oxford University Press; London, 1969). Descriptions of games current in Britain, compiled by the leading folklorists of the culture of childhood.

Frame Analysis by Erving Goffman (Harper & Row; New York, 1974). The latest of Goffman's fascinating series of essays on face-to-face interactions, this one dealing with how situations are defined.

The Psychology of Interpersonal Behaviour by Michael Argyle (Penguin Books; Harmondsworth and Baltimore, 1972). A social psychologist's view of the minutiae of human behaviour, and their relation to the practical affairs of life.

Argonauts of the Western Pacific by Bronislaw Malinowski (Routledge; London, 1922 and Dutton; New York, 1961). An anthropological classic, telling of the elucidation of the Kula exchanges and broader aspects of Trobriand life.

The Context of Social Psychology edited by J. Israel and H. Tajfel (Academic Press; New York and London, 1972). Critical essays by leading European social psychologists, who react against recent trends in their field.

Acknowledgements

Acknowledgement is due to the following for permission to reproduce illustrations:

Page 2–3, Kunsthistorisches Museum, Vienna; 17, D. Ashford's literary estate and Chatto & Windus; 18, Derry Bogert and Anthro-Photo; 21, Irven DeVore and Anthro-Photo; 22, Melvin Konner and Anthro-Photo; 25, Carl W. Rettenmeyer; 28, RTHPL; 29, Mansell Collection; 34, Sarah Landry and Harvard University; 40, Mansell Collection; 41, Mansell Collection; 42, Mansell Collection; 44, National Women's Hospital, Auckland; 48, Department of Psychology, University of Edinburgh; 54, Dr L. Robbins; 56, Department of Psychology, University of Edinburgh; 72, Ernest Cole and the John Hillelson Agency; 74, Alex Webb and the John Hillelson Agency; 75, L. S. Penrose; 80, Hughes Vassal-Gamma and the John Hillelson Agency; 85, Oslo Kommunes Kunstsamlinger Munch-Museet; 87, John Gay; 88, BBC; 89, BBC; 90, John Gay; 93 *(top)*, Kunsthistorisches Museum, Vienna; 94, BBC; 96, BBC; 103, Kunsthistorisches Museum, Vienna; 113, 115, 116, Jerry Leach; 119, Graham Vaughan; 126, Marc Riboud and the John Hillelson Agency; 133, Kunsthistorisches Museum, Vienna; 134, Kunsthistorisches Museum, Vienna.

All the other photographs are by Homer Sykes. The cartoons are by Posy Simmonds.

Index

personality, 9, 13, 110–112
personas, 112
Philadelphia dialects, 130
Piaget, J., 10, 59, 61
Pidgin, 70
PKU (brain disease), 98
play, 67, 68, *69*, 101–5, 110
population control among Bushmen, 20
primates, 17–19, 23, 36, 38, 61
prisoners, personalities of, 110–112
Prisoner's Dilemma, 31, 32
promiscuity, 19
puberty, 15, 17, 112
Pusey, A. 15

Queen's Univ., Kingston, 97

racial attitudes, 29, *72*, 73–8, 86, 118–20
reality, sense of, 107–8
rebellion, 128
Rebelsky, F., 81
reciprocal altruism, 31–3, 37, 114, 124
religion, 41–3
rice, expertise about, 89–91
Richards, M., 137
riddles, 104
rituals, 102, 104, 110, 130
Rockefeller Univ., 89
role-distance, 108–9
roles, 68, 108–10, *125*

saints, villains and suckers, 31
Sander, L., 52
Sartre, J.-P., 105
schizophrenia, 84–6, 98
self, concept of, 59
selfishness, 24, 33, 136
Serbo-Croatian, 70
Serengeti National Park (Tanzania), 35
sexual differences, 15–7, 26, 27, 89–90
Shakespeare, 112
shame versus guilt, 81
Sherif, C. and M., 122
Shockley, W., 73
skin colour, 99, 109, 118
Skinner, B. F., 10
slavery, 39
Slobin, D., 70
smiling, 55
Social Darwinism, 9
social mobility versus social change, 128
Sociobiology, 23, 137
South Africa, 128
sparrows, dialects in, 131
speech, 13, 50, 51–4, 60–6, 70, 128–31, *132*
speech sounds, perception of, 50–1
squinting, 95

Stanford Univ., 15
status and discrimination, 127–8
stress, *78*, 79, 111
superstition, 104
synchrony with speech, 52
systematic personality assessment, 111

Tajfel, H., 121–7, 131–2, 137
Tanzania, 15, 35
television, 102, 108
temperament, 82–4, 109
territory control, 107
Thomas, A., 81–3
thumb-sucking, *44*, 45
'tomboy', 15
tongue, 7, 48
tonguing, imitations of, 7, 48
tools, 19, 34, 38
Torgersen, A. M., 83
torture, 29
Trevarthen, C., 55
Trivers, R., 26–33, 36, 37
Trobriand Islands, 112–8, 136
Turkish, 70
Turner, J., 127–8
twins, *75*, 83–6

'urban genes', 79
urban-rural behavioural differences, 16

Vai script, 89
Vaughan, G. 118
verbal reasoning, *16*, 17
Victoria, Queen, *28*
vision, 95–8
visual-spatial skills, 7, *16*

Waddington, C. H., 35
war, 29, 122, 128–32
Washburn, S., 43
Wells, G., 63, 64
Wiesel, T., 95
Wilson, E. O., 23, 37, 137

XYY abnormality, 73

Yanomamos, 39
Young, J. Z., 27